毕淑敏
双语美文

A Bilingual Edition of
Beautiful Stories
by Bi Shumin

U0725843

梦想不会寂寞

The Power of the Dream

毕淑敏 著

朱虹 刘海明 译

GUANGXI NORMAL UNIVERSITY PRESS
广西师范大学出版社
·桂林·

梦想不会寂寞
MENGXIANG BUHUI JIMO

出版统筹：张俊显
品牌总监：耿　磊
选题策划：耿　磊
责任编辑：土芝楠
助理编辑：韩杰文
美术编辑：卜翠红　刘冬敏
营销编辑：杜文心　钟小文
责任技编：李春林

图书在版编目（CIP）数据

　　梦想不会寂寞：汉、英 / 毕淑敏著；朱虹，刘海明
译 . 一桂林：广西师范大学出版社，2020.1
　　（毕淑敏双语美文）
　　ISBN 978-7-5598-2392-2

　　Ⅰ . ①梦… Ⅱ . ①毕…②朱…③刘… Ⅲ . ①散文集－
中国－当代－汉、英 Ⅳ . ①I267

　　中国版本图书馆 CIP 数据核字（2019）第 260448 号

广西师范大学出版社出版发行

（ 广西桂林市五里店路 9 号　邮政编码：541004 ）
　网址：http://www.bbtpress.com
出版人：黄轩庄
全国新华书店经销
保定市中画美凯印刷有限公司印刷
（保定市西三环 1566 号　邮政编码：071000）
开本：880 mm × 1 350 mm　1/32
印张：6　　字数：120 千字
2020 年 1 月第 1 版　　2020 年 1 月第 1 次印刷
印数：0 001~6 000 册　　定价：39.80 元

如发现印装质量问题，影响阅读，请与出版社发行部门联系调换。

在书中温暖相遇

几年前，广西师范大学出版社出版了我的一套书。在这套书里，我写了自己在遥远西藏的往事，写了当医生的难忘经历，写了担当心理医生时听到的故事和引发的思考……

书是缔造心灵的塑形工具。东方文化中，心并不单单指那个解剖学上的泵血器官，而是汇聚每个人的品格情操的智慧之海。有一颗仁慈之心，会爱世界爱他人爱生活，爱自身也爱大家。有一颗自强之心，会勤学苦练百折不挠，宠辱不惊大智若愚。有一颗尊严之心，会珍惜自然善待万物。有一颗流量充沛羽翼丰满的心，会乘上幻想飞船，抚摸众星的翅膀。

我遇到了朱虹老师，她就是拥有这样一颗多彩之心的睿智长者。很高兴她喜欢我书中的文字。

最初，朱虹老师想挑一些篇章翻译，作为礼物送给远在大洋彼岸的孙女外孙女们珍藏。广西师大出版社的编辑获悉这个想法，郑重邀请朱虹和刘海明老师，将本套书全部翻译出来。

这不是轻易可完成之事，是颇为繁复艰辛的工程。朱虹老师已年近90，是中国社科院德高望重的英美文学研究专家，也是一位把我国很多当代文学作品翻译介绍到国外的杰出翻译家。长期生活在国外的刘海明老师造诣高超文采斐然，和朱虹老师相得益彰珠联璧合。两位老师以醇厚学养和丰富经验，深思熟虑地将这些文字，按照英语思维方式和阅读风格，给予精彩转化，赋予它们以另外一种语言表达的鲜活生命。

补充一个小插曲。我的散文"精神的三间小屋"，被选入2018年教育部审定的全国义务教育语文教科书九年级上册。刘海明老师加班加点，将这篇文章翻译出来，收入本套书，真是雪中送炭。

面对这套双语书，我心中充盈知遇之恩和感念之情，在此向所有付出心血的老师们深表谢意！

人生是砥砺向前且充满顿挫的历程，不时筋疲力尽茫然四顾。这本小书的故事和它的成书过程，让我又一次相信，行程中有不期而至的风雨，更有美好温暖的巧遇。朱虹、海明老师和我在文字中结识，现在，我期待着——我们和你——亲爱的读者，在书中相逢。

之后，让咱们再次充满信心地出发！

2019年11月5日

When We Meet Inside a Book

A few years ago, Guangxi Normal University Press published a collection of my stories. In them, I wrote about the years I spent in remote Tibet, my unforgettable experience working as a physician, and stories and musings I gathered as a counseling psychologist.

Works of literature help shape our heart. In Eastern cultures, the heart is the sea of wisdom that nurtures our character, other than a mere organ anatomically responsible for pumping blood through the body. It is with the kind heart that one loves the world, others and life; love of oneself and all people. It is with the hardy, aspiring heart that one strives on, never giving up, and is wise, artless and unflappable. It is with the dignified heart that one cherishes nature and is kind to all creatures great and small. It is with the heart brimful of confidence that one floats on wings of imagination, touching the stars.

Then I met Zhu Hong, an erudite elder with such an unfailingly rich heart, and was most delighted that she liked the stories of this collection.

Initially, Zhu Hong had planned to translate a selection of them as a gift to be held dear by her granddaughters across the ocean. However, when the editorial staff of Guangxi Normal University Press learned about this, they decided to invite Zhu Hong and Liu Haiming to translate the entire collection into English.

It was no small undertaking, a project requiring much dedication. Zhu Hong, in her late eighties, is a venerated scholar in the field of English and American Literature with the Chinese Academy of Social Sciences. She is also noted for her incomparable translations of outstanding works of modern Chinese literature, bringing them to a wider international audience. Liu Haiming, an accomplished translator having studied and worked extensively abroad, collaborated with Zhu Hong on this project. The two scholar-translators pored over the Chinese texts and managed to bring out the spirit of the original, and give life to the stories in the English language in all its beauty and flexibility.

Incidentally, my essay "Three Little 'Rooms' for Your Soul" was selected for the 2018 edition of the Ministry of Education-approved high school textbook for Chinese Language and Literature, for the first semester of the ninth year of National Compulsory Education. Beavering away, Liu Haiming had it timely translated for inclusion in the present collection.

As this bilingual collection was ready for printing, I felt most grateful for our privileged connection. My thanks go to all who have put all the hard work into its publication.

Life is a journey, with inevitable challenges and setbacks, which, at times, can wear you out, and loneliness captures you. Yet, for all the storms out of the blue, there are also fortuitous, heartening encounters along the way—a belief borne out by the stories in this collection and its publication. Zhu Hong, Haiming and I met in the pages of these stories, and now I look forward to our encounter with you, dear readers, in this little collection.

Then, brimful of confidence again, we will journey on!

Bi Shumin, November 5, 2019

contents
目 录

contents
目 录

成功十二条——知道并不等于能做到

如何达到成功?

成功等于目标的实现。设定好了目标，就要开始行动了。这是一个非常显而易见的道理，几乎所有的朋友都知道，但知道并不等于行动。如果把目标只停留在豪言壮语的阶段，或者是写在本子上，却不能落实在行动中，那么所有的成功计划都是画饼充饥。

最诚实的措施就是要坚持到底、永不放弃，但这也并不等于说有了坚持的精神，就一定会成功。成功不是外在的评价，而是内心的感受。

一个人在争取成功的过程中，享受到了精神的高度和心境的愉悦。如果享有了这些，最终的成败并不是最重要的，因为你已经成功了。

所以，找到你真正的兴趣所在，这是非常重要的第一条。

真正的兴趣是什么，要靠你自己的摸索、思考、探索，这是一个饶有兴趣但也很茫然的过程。只有找到了你真正的兴趣所在，然后致力于这个领域，你才有可能找到走向成功的那条最近的道路。道理很简单，如果这是你的长项，你就会有使不完的劲儿，层出不穷的新鲜点子，就会在遇到挫败的时候依旧兴致盎然。而这些，都是成功的好伴侣。

第二条是建立起良好的人际关系。

现代社会高速发展，再不是单枪匹马的小农时代，你闷头耕地就一了百了。成功不仅仅是个人的事情，而是和整个时代的脉搏紧密相连。良好的人际关系，是加速成功的强大助力。每一个渴望成功的人都不要闭关锁国。

第三条是永远不要期待不劳而获。

我们常常会听到许多成功者受"贵人"相助的故事，包括一夜暴富的神话，都会讲得有鼻子有眼，叫你不得不相信。

这个世界上一定有匪夷所思的奇迹，但更多的是持之以恒的努力和珍珠一样的汗水，脚踏实地、日复一日地在一块土地上耕耘。只要你的种子是优良的、你的方法得当，那么即使第一年遇到风，第二年遇到雨，第三年遇到冰雹，第四年遇到蝗虫，我们仍然有理由继续期待丰收。即使在所有的岁月中都没有金黄的谷穗，你付出的劳动，大地也会收藏。

第四条也不能忘，那就是知道在做什么的同时，也牢记不应该做什么。很多时候，我们会遭遇诱惑，特别是求索成功的攀登中，几乎处处潜伏着不正当手段化装成的毒蛇。它们扮出笑脸对我们说，和我一道吧，我知道一条偏僻的小路，包你可以更快地到达顶峰。如果你一动心，被蛊惑，走上崎岖的小道，等待你的就不是顶峰的旖旎风光，而很可能是悬崖峭壁。成功不仅仅是结果，更是过程。结果可能在世俗的目光中并不辉煌，但我们自心欣慰。

下一个要记住的是——要有计划。

很多人习惯眉毛胡子一把抓，成天忙忙碌碌以为日子充实而饱满，以为所有的努力都是在为成功添砖加瓦。殊不知计划是向导，按照事先列出的明确、细致的计划去做，就像将军战役前准备地图，这是必不可少的功课。有计划的人和没有计划的人之间的分别，在一两个月的时间可能看得不大分明，但一两年就一定会有令人惊讶不已的差距，十年数十年卜来，呈现出天壤之别。

第六条，要有创新。

这是一个很简单却常常被别人忽略的原则。

想想看，你期冀成功的领域已经有千百万人反复思谋探索过，好似被游览了若干年的公园。如果你没有一点属于自己的独创的闪光点，你如何能脱颖而出呢？压榨你的大脑吧，它具有强大的潜能。据说人的大脑可能产生三十亿个创想，这是一个了不起的数字。人脑就像一匹骏马，在好骑手的驾驭下，它会像一道闪电掠过草原，速度之快，超乎所有人的想象。

第七条，请超越自己。

当你取得了一定的成就时，超越自己就成了常常要对自己说的一句话。也许，超越别人还是比较容易的事情，由不得你放松，由不得你懈怠。但是，当你到了"一览众山小"的高度，继续成功的强大阻力，有时候就来自你的故步自封。

在成功的游泳中，你要不间断地劈风斩浪，每当你对自己有了新的突破之时，你就又向成功的彼岸逼近了一步。

第八条有点老生常谈，那就是珍惜时间。

如果把成功比作一幅锦缎，那么分分秒秒就是织就这幅锦缎的丝线。你放弃丝线就是自毁了华美的锦缎。再伟大的恒星也不过是一些元素的组合，你的生命就是由看似漫不经心、无声无息的分秒集合而成的。在获取成功的列车运动图上，要有只争朝夕的精神。

如果你是一个渴望成功的人，就请认真地想想时间这个坐标系。秒针"嘀嘀答答"重复运行，错觉主宰着我们，仿佛时间取之不尽用之不竭。要想充分领悟时间的宝贵，就需要把参照物放大。

你如果想把握光年的长度，请看银河。

你如果想把握沧海桑田的长度，请看化石。

你如果想把握一生的长度，请看墓园。

你如果想把握一年的长度，请看麦田。

你如果把握一个月的长度，请看婴孩。

你如果想把握一天的长度，请看潮起潮落。

你如果想把握一个小时的长度，请看抢救心脏。

你如果想把握一分钟的长度，请看上班族的打卡。

你如果想把握一秒钟的长度，请看神舟飞船升天。

你如果想把握一毫秒的长度，请看奥运健儿百米争冠。

你如果想把握自己一生的长度，请珍惜眼前无数个瞬间。

第九条，是不惧怕失败。

谁要说你一定能成功，请不要相信，无论他是出于怎样的善意。

谁要说你一定会有失败，请一定相信，不管他是出于怎样的狭隘动机。

谁要是说你如果能从失败中汲取经验教训，就会向成功迫近，这句话就几乎是真理了。

你追求的成功越是高远，你遭遇的失败就越是顺理成章。在这个问题上，不要以为自己是命运的宠儿，可以不经历风霜之苦，就得到梅花之香。

善待每一次失败，把它给予的痛苦珍藏，经过发酵，酿出佳酿，保存在成功的酒窖里。

第十条，务必认真对待小事。

这里所说的小事，是那种可能积累成大事的小事，不是真正的鸡毛蒜皮。人一生当中，有一些是纯粹的小事，一个渴望成功的人，是不可以长久地关注在这种小事之上，那会像酸雨一样磨损了你的意志，耗费了你的时间，直到最后，把你销蚀成一个浑浑噩噩的庸人。

有一些小事，就像巴西热带雨林里一只蝴蝶的翅膀颤动，有可能引发纽约华尔街的地震，你切莫麻痹大意，埋藏下隐患。有一句歌词叫作"给我一双慧眼吧"，据说原本是为了打击假冒伪劣商品而作，后来被人们广为传唱。只是慧眼恐怕不是什么人或是老天爷能给你的，只有靠自己的磨炼和积累，不断地擦拭。

第十一条，很简单，就两个字——顽强。

追求成功的过程中会遇到很多艰难、困苦、挫折与失败。你不打败它们，它们就会打败你。你可以被打败一次，也可以被打败多次，但只要你有顽强的意志，有不屈不挠的精神，你就可以坚持到最后。

那时，也许你仍然无法得到世俗意义上的成功，但是在精神上，你已经把成功的花冠挽在手中。

第十二条，还是两个字——坚持。

你确立了自己的方向之后，再没有什么比坚持这种品性，更朴素但又更恒久地为你提供能量了。水滴石穿、粒米成箩，不积跬步无以至千里……讲的都是这个道理。

不要小看了坚持，能坚持的人和不能坚持的人，结果天壤之别。你可以选择一曝十寒，或是持之以恒，当你做这种选择的时候，实际上你已经决定了自己的成功与否。

除此之外，还请记得礼貌待人，乐于助人，做事有条理，保持心情舒畅，真诚对待自己，真诚对待他人，不要自我哀怜，乐于赞扬他人，热爱学习……

看到这里，你可能会说：怎么都是些人人皆知的大道理啊？这些话，我们从小到大都听了几百遍了，有很多条在幼儿园就学过了。是的，这些基本的道理是我们从小就知道的，但是，你知道了，并不等于你记住了。你记住了，也并不等于你就能够照着去做。

只有当这些人类最基本的美德成为你内心结构的一部分，甚至融化在你的血液中，也就是进入了你的心理底层，架构起你思维的地基，你才能更快地走向成功。

如此这般，你不用处心积虑地寻找成功了，成功会一步一步地向你走过来，如同你站在巨轮的甲板上，有扑面而来的风。

12 Rules of Success — and Action

What is the secret to success?

Success means achieving one's goal. You define your aim and take action. Plain and simple. Most will agree, yet not everyone follows through. Ambitious goals, even if you've had them boisterously declared or jotted down in your little journal, will amount to little more than a pie in the sky, elusive as long as you don't get your hands dirty working towards them.

Work honestly, too; with perseverance and grit, even though tenacity alone does not guarantee success.

Success also has more to do with your innate sense of

fulfilment, than accolades from others. As you are bold in the glory of mission and joy of purposeful endeavour, the fact you have strived is success enough, while the reward of outcome only accessory.

Thus, rule No. 1: Identify your true passion.

It requires, on your part, much soul-searching, hard-thinking and exploration; a process both fascinating and painstaking. You are most likely to be successful when you commit efforts to what you love. Find your calling and you will work untiringly, with boundless creative energy. No setbacks dampen your inexhaustible drive.

Rule No. 2: Build good interpersonal relationships.

We have come a long way from the agrarian age when a farmer ploughing a lonely furrow could be self-sufficient all by himself. Success in our rapidly changing society is not merely about doing the best job you can, but also how to best work with others in an interconnected world. Sound interpersonal relationships are hugely conducive to success. Never shut yourself off, if you ever want to be successful in your endeavours.

Rule No. 3: No pains, no gains.

We often hear tales of those who have succeeded thanks to a certain magnanimous patronage. There are also rags-to-riches stories, too, of those who made it single-handedly — all made out to be realistic and convincing.

Miracles do happen, incredulous though they seem. Yet, what we see most often in the world is the persistent, unyielding work of all those bringing in the harvest season after season by the sweat of their brows. As long as you put down good seeds and tend to them the proper way, you have ample reason to expect a good harvest. You might be set back by storm, excessive rain, hail, or locust infestation. Yet, year after year the work you put in will improve and enrich the soil, even though for all your hard work.

Rule No. 4: Know what not to do.

When we struggle to reach our goal and continuously scale new heights, shenanigans in the disguise of convenient shortcuts, promising a quicker approach to the summit will tempt us. In our momentary bewilderment and weakness, we may be led to a tortuous path to the precipice of doom, instead of a peak with breathtaking vistas. Beware and know what not to do. Success is not only about a winsome outcome, but the process of achieving it. We should still feel richly rewarded for our strife, even though an outcome is judged less than glorious by conventional wisdom.

Rule No. 5: Have a plan.

Many feel quite content when being busy. With a finger in every pie, they believe their day is not in vain. Being up to their eyeballs in multiple efforts gives them their sense of success. Yet, little do they know they would be much better off by having a specific, well-laid-out plan first, like a general plotting his campaign on a map — indispensable to victory. The difference between someone with a well-thought-out plan and those without becomes apparent in a matter of years, if not months. Over a decade or two, there will be a world of difference between the lives of the well-planned and the plan-not.

Rule No. 6: Be innovative.

It may seem that this goes without saying, simple and self-evident, but it is often neglected.

If your chosen field of endeavour happens to be the same as those of countless others — a crowded path, so to speak — you will have to be inventive, to think out of the box, in order to be outstanding. Put your brain, the organ with the greatest potential, to work. It is said that the human brain is capable of producing three billion ideas in a normal lifespan, which is truly amazing. Train your brain and harness its power; miraculous and dazzling, fast as lightning, like the finest steed shooting across rolling pasture.

Rule No. 7: Conquer self.

Once you have attained a certain level of

success, you will come to the realization that beating the competition is not all that difficult, though it may have required diligence and persistent efforts. When you have outdone everyone else, the challenge is to outdo yourself, for the greatest obstacle to your further success will come from you — your self-conceit and complacency.

You need to overcome your own limitations to excel, like endurance swimmers who must beat their inner fears to triumph over waves and swells, to reach the "Golden Shore."

Rule No. 8: Don't squander time.

If success is a tapestry, time will be the threads woven in its splendour. Any minute wasted diminishes it. Your entire lifetime is composed of the seemingly insignificant minutes and hours, unnoticeably and ceaselessly passing. In striving to make the best of yourself, seize the day!

If you yearn for success in life, don't overlook the time dimension. Don't be misled by the illusion that time is infinite, and is all yours for the taking, as though each tick-tock but a repetition. For a point of reference, consider the following:

The sweep of galaxies is measured by light-years,

The march of geological eons by fossils and minerals.

A lifetime on a headstone, a year's travail in a single crop;

The passing of months in the progress of an infant;

And the passing of a day in the ebb and flow of tides;

You see the preciousness of an hour when saving a heart patient, a minute at punch-in and punch-out as a wage-earner, a second in the launch of a rocket, and a millisecond in winning the 100-meter sprint.

You must seize the moment, seize the day, to get the most out of your life.

Rule No. 9: Do not fear failure.

Never believe anyone who says you will not

fail, despite their good intentions. Believe those who say failure is inevitable, no matter how mean they may seem. If someone tells you that by learning from your failure you will get closer to success, that's an approximation to the truth.

The loftier your goal, the more likely you will encounter setbacks. Never delude yourself into thinking you can be the favoured one, enjoying the sweet smell of success without trials and failure.

Treat each failure as treasure, for they are essential to success, though they may be bitter, like ingredients for brewing a delectable libation. They are to be cherished.

Rule No. 10: Pay attention to the nitty-gritty.

By nitty-gritty, I mean elements capable of major consequences, rather than trivialities that distract us in life. Never let the latter get in the way, if you intend to achieve your goal, for they will erode your force of will, bog you down, and reduce you to a dispirited dawdler; as acid rain decimates the forest.

Yet details that appear insignificant can cause serious

consequences, as the proverbial butterfly fluttering its wings in the Amazon jungle may wreak havoc on Wall Street. You neglect them at your peril. "Lend me your eagle eye," as a line in the once popular song goes. The song was meant for combating counterfeits, but later took on a wider meaning. However, no one can make you more discerning; nor is it a naturally endowed ability. It can only be acquired through learning and constant honing.

Rule No. 11: Be tenacious.

As you strive to achieve your goal, you are likely to encounter difficulties, hardships, setbacks and failures along the way. You either overcome them or be defeated by them, and repeatedly so, as the case may be. You fight with tenacity, never give up, and endure to the end. You are a winner no less, even though success by conventional definitions still eludes you; for spiritually you have overcome the worst that life can throw at you.

Rule No. 12: Be persistent.

Once you have set your goal, perseverance, above all else, sustains you in your drive to achieve it. Ancient adages expounding such a notion abound: "Constant dripping of water wears away the stone;" "Mighty oaks from little acorns grow;" and "The journey of a thousand miles begins with the first step."

This is never a trivial trait. Perseverance, or the lack of it, makes a world of difference. You can choose to be persistent or work by fits and starts, which really means the difference between success and failure.

In addition, remember also to be courteous, organized, helpful and cheerful. Be true to yourself and others. Refrain from self-pity, be quick to praise, and eager to learn...

Well then, you might say, all these are but common sense. You have heard them umpteen times, many of which in kindergarten. Indeed, they are simple rules that we may have known since we were little. Yet, it doesn't necessarily follow that you have taken them to heart. Even if you do, you may not have put them into action.

It is only when these essential human virtues become part of you — somethings that run in your blood, form the foundation of your soul, and kindle your passion, will you be truly successful in life.

Only then, success that has eluded you will come your way. You plow ahead having the wind at your back, like a ship sailing with a following sea.

你的身体里必有一颗成功的种子

在每个人的生命里，都有一个关于创造的秘密，等待着被发现。那将是你的第二次诞生。

你一定要相信，在你的身体里，有一颗种子，焦灼地盼望着阳光。至于它到底是一颗什么种子，在没有发芽之前，谁也不知道。

你的责任就是给它浇水，保护它不被鸟雀啄食，不因为干渴而失去生机，不会被人偷走，也不会在你饥肠辘辘的时刻被你炒熟了充饥。如果那样做了，你虽可一时果腹，却丧失了长久发展的原动力。

那颗种子可能藏在你的耳朵里，你就有灵敏的听觉。可能藏在你的手指甲里，你就有非凡的触觉。也可能在你的眸子里，也可能在你的肌肉中。当然了，更可能在你的大脑中、心脏里、双手中……

每个人在属于个人的成长经历中，早已获得了解决问题的丰富宝藏。请信任我们的潜意识，它必定能在正确的时机产生恰当的回应。告诉你一句悄悄话——有时候，信息也将以非语言的方式揭露真相。

找找吧。一定找得到！

身体里绝对有不少于一百种的功能，能保证你在浑然不觉中完成种种复杂的运作。但你不要以为这些功能会一直老老实实地待在那里，它们是勤勤恳恳的，却不是任劳任怨的。如果你一直视它们的存在为理所当然，从来不照料它们，不维护和激励它们，或是过度使用，或置若罔闻，那么，它们不是反抗，就是消极怠工，也许会集体突围，无声无息地溜走了，然而你误以为它们从来不曾居住在你的身体里。要知道，一辈子无意识地随波逐流，会导致你各种功能的退化。

成功并不像想象的那样难。因为我们不敢做，它才变得难起来。

There Must Be a Seed of Success in You

Our life is miraculous. There is a myth to be deciphered; there is a seed lying deep within each of us, yearning for the light to germinate, to begin a new you. Have faith, for no one knows what such seeds may be, until seedlings grow and legends bloom.

The duty for cultivating your seedling falls upon you — water it, feed it, keep the birds and bugs away, and guard it against pilferage. You may be tempted to harvest it prematurely to satisfy your hunger. Guard against that also, or you will destruct its full potential.

The seed may be the gift of an exceptional ear for music,

deft fingers of exquisite sensitivity, extraordinary sight, or powerful muscles. Most likely, of course, it may be your blessed brains, heart or hands...

As we live our lives, we acquire the experience of solving problems that come our way. Such experiences are valuable treasures. Trust the subconscious; it will provide the proper response at the right moment. And truth can be divined in non-verbal terms.

Never stop your search and self-discovery!

Your body is capable of no fewer than one hundred physiological functions; complex reflexes and actions performed without your being consciously aware of them. They are highly effective, yet require honing and nurturing. Your body will resist and revolt, with these functions deserting you altogether, if you take them for granted, without caring for them, or keeping them from abuse and neglect. You begin to doubt if they have ever existed. They may also denigrate, if they remain unused, as you live life always going with the flow, never putting yourself to the test.

Success is not as difficult to attain, as you may have thought. It becomes elusive when you refuse to try and dare not take the plunge.

放弃不等于失败

放弃争夺，并不是拱手让别人赢，只是舍去和远离。我不和你们赛跑，并不表示自己的失败，只是说明我们没有开始比赛。

人生似乎离不开比赛，但其实，人生根本就不是比赛，你和谁都不需要比。如果一定要找到对手，那就是死亡，但结局已经注定，所以，这也不是比赛，只是过程。承认在某些问题上的无能为力，你反而可以把更多的力量，投入真正可以取得成效的领域。

我年轻的时候，常常羞于说出自己已黔驴技穷。

我总想挣扎，总以为凭着自己不懈的努力，可以扭转乾坤。现在，我这样坚持的时候越来越少了。我常常退却，因为我知道一己微弱，有时要暂时偃旗息鼓，但我不会放弃，不过是换了另外一种节奏的步伐。

放弃并不等于失败，因为你没有参加比赛，所以那个结果与你无干。但放弃也不等于成功，因为你缺席了，结果是躲避和退让。如果是一次，可以算作一个策略；如果常常如此，你实际上就是放弃多彩的人生。

人的一生，不能不放弃。一次都不放弃的人生，是不现实的。起码，你最后一次是要放弃生命，你不想放弃也不行，有自然规律管着呢，在这之前，你还曾放弃过青春，放弃过健康，也可能放弃过理想，放弃过亲人……不管你喜欢还是不喜欢，你必须放弃。

放弃是个强有力的席卷者，最后会将我们所有的一切都打包带走。所以，学会和放弃和平共处吧。你越早学会，越受益无穷。因为放弃不是失败，只是一个阶段。

随着年龄的增长，我们的生命越来越由我们的选择来塑造。你活得越久，你的选择就越多，你越要小心地做出决定。但是，也不可事事都放弃，你不能总是这样，那是懦夫和懒汉的哲学。

To Let Go Is No Defeat

When you quit a feud, it doesn't mean surrender. Throw in the towel and opt for the edge — it is a matter of choice. Refrain from the race and you suffer no loss, for to you the race has yet to start.

Life may seem like an endless race. Yet, in truth, life is not a race — you needn't race against anyone. If you ultimately must run against something, it will be death. Yet, such an end is predetermined and thus a process to be precise, not a race. As we recognize our powerlessness against such a fateful process, we can then be better focused on and devote ourselves to achieving plausible goals.

When I was young, I was ashamed to admit my own limitations, that I was by and large a one-trick-pony. I was doggedly convinced that I could change the world as long as I tried hard enough. Nowadays, I have less and less that sort of pluckiness. Knowing how feeble one's efforts can be, I have resorted to a different pace. Though I will never give up my endeavours, I pause from time to time for reprieve.

Quitting does not mean failure, for you are no longer in the race and thus have nothing to do with its outcome — nor does it mean success. It may serve as a useful strategy once in a while. Yet if you keep doing this, you'd be giving up any chance to live a rich, colourful life.

No one goes through life without ever quitting. It is simply impossible that you never let go of anything. To say the very least, you will eventually let go of your own life — an end determined by the law of nature. Before that finale, you will have let go of your youthfulness, health, and possibly your cherished dream and your loved ones... You must have let go one way or the other, like it or not.

When you let go, you let it be all swept way. And ultimately, so will we let go everything that once we have to our name. Therefore, learn to live with having to let go; the earlier, the better, from which you will benefit infinitely. Letting go is but the end of a phase of phases.

As we get on in age, our life becomes increasingly the product of our choices. The longer you live, the more options you will have and the more careful you should be with your selections. However, you should certainly not end up letting go and calling it quits every time you find yourself in a jam. If you do, you would be nothing more than a stoic quitter and timorous layabout.

31

闭阖星云之眼

青年时代，我曾经有一段时间是一个悲观主义者，这也许是和我在西藏高原的经历有关。高原太辽阔了，人力太渺小了。雪峰太久远了，人生太短暂了。有时真是生出无尽的悲哀，觉得奋斗有什么用呢？百年之后，不还是一抔黄土？一个人的力量太微薄了，太平洋不会因为一杯沸水的倾倒而升高温度，这杯水却永远地消失了。

后来，我知道这种看世界的角度被哲学家称为"星云"或"银河之眼"。从这个位置来看，我们和目所能及的所有生物都是微不足道，一切奋斗都显得荒凉和愚蠢，结局和发展都充满了不可言说的荒谬。一个人，和一只蚂蚁、一条蛆虫没有任何分别。从星云和银河的角度来看，人类轻渺如烟、无足挂齿。

这只眼振振有词，在逻辑上几乎是无懈可击的。你若真要遵循了这只眼的视角，会从根本上使生命枯萎凋落。

一些好高骛远的人，在遭受失败的时候，会拾起这只眼为自己开脱。因为所有的努力和小努力都混为一谈，他的失败也就顺理成章。一些胸无大志的人，在沉沦和荒靡的时刻，会躲在这只眼后面为自己寻找借口。因为一切都在虚无中，他的荒废光阴也就有了理论支点。一些游戏人生放弃光明的人，在黑暗中也眨巴着这只眼，似乎一切都是梦，清醒和昏迷并无分别……

你不要小看了这看似遥远而又神秘的星云之眼，如果你长期用这只眼注视世界，就会不由自主地灰心丧志。持久地沉浸其中，还有可能放弃生命。当我们从生活中抽离，成为袖手旁观的旁观者时，所有世俗的欢快和目标，就变得轻如鸿毛。

闭阖星云之眼吧。因为那不是你的位置，那是神的位置。摒弃那高处不胜寒的孤寂，回到充满生机又复杂多变的人间吧。僭越是危险的，我们今生为人，是一种福气。珍惜我们明察秋毫的双眼，可以仰视星空，却不要让自己轻飘飘地飞起来，到达星云的高度。那里，据说很冷、很黑、很荒凉。

那些让我们感到有内涵、有勇气、有坚持力的人，我坚信他们是有理想的。人很怪，只有理想这种东西，才能够提供源源不断的动力。

Come off the Perch of the Cosmic View

In my youth, for quite a while I was a pessimist, which perhaps had something to do with my experience on the Tibetan Plateau. Reflecting on its unfathomable vastness and its timeless snow-capped peaks, I was at times seized with bottomless despair at the insignificance of humanity's power, the fickleness of life, and the futility of personal endeavours — all to be reduced to little more than a fistful of dust when one's life is over. An individual's efforts, no matter how strenuous, are feeble; like a glass of warm water that is instantly lost when poured into the ocean, with no effect whatsoever on its overall temperature.

I was to learn that this sort of worldview is what philosophers refer as the cosmic view. From this perspective, we and all living things visible in our vision are insignificant and infinitesimal, human enterprise obscure and utter folly, and cosmic progression and all endings inexplicably absurd. We are not much different from ants and maggots, and humanity ethereal and barely a blip on the cosmic timescale.

Such a perspective carries the apparent force of logic, seemingly unassailable. Yet, should you take it to heart, your life would only diminish and wither.

Some adopt this perspective when they fail to achieve their lofty, unrealistic goals; taking solace in the inevitability of setbacks of all inconsequential human efforts. The less ambitious adopt this view so as to take cover under a philosophical pretext, relishing their insolence and inaction. Faced with the prospect of universal nihilism and void of meaning, it's even philosophically advisable to dally. The cynically facetious, squinting in the dark with a dim view of the world, and given to thinking that life is but a dream and there is no real difference between reverie and reality, also embrace this view.

Yet we should be wary of such a cosmic stance, albeit mystic and surreal. If you look at the world unceasingly with such a view, it will depress your spirit, crush your pride, and eventually cause your self-destruction, if you cannot pull yourself out of its soulless depth. As we become detached, sitting on our hands like outsiders looking on, life with all its humdrum tasks and joys becomes insignificant, not worth a straw.

So stop dwelling on that sort of cosmic standpoint. It is really for the gods, not you. Trade the despairing solitude of the haughty perch for the world of everyday human existence; vibrant, perplexing and ever changing. Being earthly is truly a blessing while assuming the cosmic stance can be perilous and transgressing. Cherish our sharp eyes as we admire the starry, starry sky; yet guard against the urge to float up to the heaven's door, to command the cosmic view. Up there, so it is said, is dark, desolate, and cold in the extreme.

We gravitate toward the salt of the earth — men and women of substance, resolve and endurance; for they never compromise on their ideals, which, oddly, are the only perennial wellspring of human energy.

不真实不现实的工作

世界上很少有报酬丰厚却不需要承担巨大责任的便宜事。

记得我曾跟一些上中学的孩子谈心，他们尚年幼，我以为对各自的将来还懵懵懂懂。不想，大谬。几乎每个孩子，都能振振有词地把将来的工作阐述一番。让我吃惊的是，他们向往的职位，都是挣钱多而轻松惬意，且不想负担很大的责任。

我不知道这种想法从何而来，估计是周围的成人灌输给他们的吧。我以为，这是一种不良的期待。

第一，这不真实。世界上有没有挣得多、活儿又轻松的事呢？我不敢说绝对没有，但我敢说，概率一定非常低。如果大家都想找这样的事，那几乎轮不到你头上。依我多年来的经验，在你考虑问题的时候，对那些小概率事件干脆不要打到算盘里，因为太容易碰壁，到那时你会埋怨社会的不公平。其实，是你先对这种可能性的概率失去了公平的判断。

第二，这不现实。现实是，这基本上是个付出劳动才能获得收益的世界。我见过付出了劳动却得不到收益的事，这种事还真不算少。于是便有了这样的说法：只问耕耘，不问收获。为什么不问呢？因为没法问，问了，那回答也不乐观，收获很可能是零。因为你做事的过程中，你收获了喜悦，乐在其中，也就物有所值。总而言之，你干活得不到报酬的事，常常发生。反过来的事，几乎没有。你说现实残酷也罢，不讲理也罢，它就是这样一板一眼，自说自话。

第三，行业中有许多秘密你不知道。你看到的只是表面现象，为什么别人可以得到既风光、收入又好的工作？当事人不一定把所有的秘密都告诉你。看似风光的外表下，往往隐藏着许多不为人知的艰辛。

写在这里，是想提醒那些期望少干活多拿钱的人，及早放弃这个念头。不然的话，徒生烦恼和痛苦。

A Plum Job

A plum job that involves little responsibility for much money must be as rare as hen's teeth.

I remember the conversation I had with a bevy of high school students. I had thought they would have very little idea of what the future had in store for them, since they were so young. However, I was wrong. To my surprise, each of them articulated what their future jobs would be like with braggadocio. Without exception, they aspired to jobs that are well-paid, comfortable and not involving a lot of responsibility.

I had no clue where they had all got their ideas. Perhaps they had been force-fed by adults around them. To me, these were rather unwholesome expectations.

To start with, they are highly improbable. I wouldn't say there are absolutely no cushy jobs in the real world. If there are, they will be few and far between, and highly sought after, and the likelihood of your landing one next to zero. Speaking from my own experience over the years, I don't believe they should be in the equation at all when you plan for your future, lest your ego be bruised, which would leave you fuming about how unfair the world is. In fact, you have yourself to blame for not having a fair assessment in the first place.

Second, they are unrealistic. By and large, you are only rewarded for the work you put in. I have seen those who have worked without getting any pay, which is hardly rare. Then, there are those who claim to care more about work than reward. Well, it might well be that their reward is so disappointing and amounting to pittance, in light of the efforts they put in. Yet, by deriving joy from their work, they still feel rewarded. In short, work without pay occurs regularly while the reverse almost never. You may think it cruel and the world tyrannous, yet that is the way it is regardless how you wish.

Third, there is so much in the world of work that you don't know. What you may have seen is the mere surface. Why can someone get a glamorous and highly-paid job? Those in the know may not necessarily be ready to blab out the secrets. You see the veneer, but not the untold struggle and sorrow.

In conclusion, my advice to those wishing to get good pay without much exertion: you'd better abandon such an idea as quickly as you can, or else you would be mightily disappointed.

溪水金沙

人的天性如溪水，学习的本能就是金沙。它们潜伏在水中，浪花翻溅时一眼看不到它的颗粒，但因它们的存在，水变得更有分量和价值。

我相信那些不含有金沙的小溪已经干涸，因为人类生存的环境曾经并且还将是刺骨险恶，你一个人的经历是不丰富的，你同时代的借鉴是不全面的，你一个行业的规则是不完整的……如果不爱学习、不善于学习、不坚持学习的话，就会被层出不穷的打击和灾变征伐与掩埋，这个人的遗传基因就昙花一现地湮灭了。

所以，乐观地说，我们每个人都是那些爱学习的人的后代，唯有这项潜藏在血液中的专擅，令我们比所有的动物都更繁荣递进。

学习是有很多种方法的，比如抬头望天，你可以学到星空的叙事是无与伦比的宏大，滋生出的渺小和畏惧感让你一生警醒、谦逊。比如低头俯地，你可以窥到万物葱茏、物竞天择、优胜劣汰、残酷、公平，激发出的紧迫和危机感让你不敢有一刻懈怠与放松。比如听妈妈讲那过去的事情，你会生出无限的柔情，不但绕指，更是绕心。比如看风光大片、科幻影像，你会惊骇莫名，有一种充满未知的狂喜和震撼……

然而，我以为最好的学习还是阅读。

首先我们要感谢文字，因为有了文字，我们的情感血脉才有了附着的骨骼，我们的理论枝蔓才有了攀缘的篱笆，我们的科技成果才有了传袭的衣钵，我们的历史才有了一面面古镜矗立照耀。

时代进步，从布帛竹简到计算机液晶屏，书写变得越来越快，阅读变得越来越方便了。记得我小时候，看一本长篇小说要个把星期，那还算快的呢！借书给朋友，不过百八十页，半个月后要她还，她说，这才几天啊你就催，我还没看完呢，小气呀小气！

读书，一种是技艺之书，讲的是各行各业的特殊规则；还有一种是普遍的知识，比如文史哲。读行业之书的人多，读普遍知识的人少。有一年我到国内著名的一所医科大学授课，我说，你们这些未来中国最杰出的医生，有谁读过《红字》？有谁读过《罪与罚》？请举手。台下抬臂者寥寥。在感谢了这些博士生的诚实之后，我深表遗憾。一个医生，除了读医书以外，也要读艺术。因为你面对的不是一只装满了病痛脓血的破罐子，而是一个活生生的人。生死契阔啊，他们在最悲苦无助的时候和你狭路相逢，你要医治他，不仅仅是凭着你的精湛医术，更要凭着你强大的人格和综合的力量。如果你想当一个名医而非庸医，请在读医书的同时也展读人文科学方面的书籍。提高了你的素养，是你的福气，是你爹妈、妻子、丈夫、孩子的福气，同时也造福了你的病患。

我相信，一个读过很多专业以外书籍的建筑师盖出的楼房一定更漂亮、更实用。我相信，一个读过很多专业以外书籍的学者，授课传业的时候一定更风趣、更幽默、旁征博引、口吐莲花。我相信，一个读过很多专业以外书籍的科学家，提出的设想和理论一定更曲径通幽、独树一帜。我相信，一个读过很多专业以外书籍的管理者，企业一定更具活力和创新精神。

我们曾经有过阅读备感艰难的时代。高玉宝的"我要读书"就是明证。那时候的无法阅读，是因为贫困和压迫。

现如今，很多人不再贫穷，也没有人压制阅读，可时间成了瓶颈，很多人苦恼的是总也找不到空闲来阅读。

那是因为有太多的诱惑。

阅读是没有香氛的，于是抵不过餐桌的美味。阅读是孤独的，于是没有觥筹交错的热闹。阅读是伴有思考和停顿的，于是没有游戏般的顺畅和惬意。阅读甚至是充满碰撞和痛楚的，因为有忏悔的顾盼和掘进的深入。

但是，优秀的阅读是有力量的，因为在阅读的时候，你不是一个人，而是和古今中外的先驱者们并行。

The Drive to Learn

Of all attributes that define the essence of humanness, the drive to learn is the most precious, like gold in the sandy sediments of a gurgling stream that glimmers when gravel and sand is washed away. Gold deposits heightens a stream value; the drive to learn our humanity.

The river of humanity would have long dried up if not for such an inherent drive. Our species have faced and will continue to face daunting challenges in our quest for survival. An individual's experience is never sufficient, without being augmented by learning from others beyond his mere contemporaries and fellow humans in similar pursuits. Those not taking to, or being deft and persistent at, learning were doomed to perish in ceaseless destruction by natural calamity or war. Buried, their genes did not get the chance to be passed along.

We are thus all descendants of avid learners. It is their drive to learn that has allowed our species to thrive and prosper, better than all other animal species.

Learning takes many forms. Stargazers learn to appreciate the infinite enormity of the cosmos, acquiring a sense of awe and recognizing individual insignificance, which underline their humility and lifelong intellectual curiosity. Studying the earth, you learn plant life, evolution, survival of the fittest, and natural justice, becoming all the more keen and diligent, with a sense of urgency and foreboding. Listening to your mom spinning yarns about her childhood, too, makes your heart grow fonder. Sci-fi or blockbuster movies with spectacular settings may shake you to the core and inspire you to explore…

However, in my mind, reading is still the best way to learn.

We must be thankful to those who invented writing, with

which our feelings find expression in physical and lasting media, our musings are set down in ordered form, our inventions passed along in descriptive detail, and our histories recorded like mirrors — making us introspect and throwing light on our future.

We have come a long way in enhancing the ease of writing and reading — from the ancient bamboo slips, silk scrolls to the modern-day computer screen. Reading a novel would take up at least a week back in my time. You would be roundly accused of being stingy, if you lend a friend a book of a hundred or so pages and demanded its return in a fortnight.

When it comes to books, you have on one hand the technical or academic tomes that run the gamut of practical skills and specialized knowledge, and, on the other, general interest titles that cover for example, literature, history and philosophy. On balance, there are more readers of books of various fields of study than those of general interest books. Some years ago, I taught classes at a well-known Chinese medical college. Once I asked the class of future medical practitioners if any of them had read *The Scarlet Letter* or *Crime and Punishment*. Few raised their hands. I thanked them all for their candour, and told them my deep disappointment. I pointed out that being future doctors, they should also read books about art and humanities, in addition to medical textbooks, for they would be interacting with human beings, not mere clinical cases with symptoms of pain, pus and bleeding. They would be treating patients who came, in their most sorrowful and helpless state, and their help might mean the difference between life and death. This called for not only superb medical skills, but also force of character and well-rounded personality. If they aspired to become outstanding doctors, rising above mediocrity, they should really read up on canons of the humanities in addition to being well versed in medicine. Only then will they really have a shot at being a doctor of superior calibre, benefiting their patients tremendously and bringing accolades to themselves, their parents, spouse, and offspring.

I am convinced that houses designed by a well-read architect will have a greater beauty to form and function. A well-read lecturer will surely be more amusing in his presentation that is spiced up with extensive anecdotes, keeping his class in stitches with his endless wisecracks. A well-read scientist will tend to think out-of-the-box and have a trail-blazing rigor in advancing new ideas. A business with a well-read leader will surely be more robust and innovative.

We once lived in an era where books were hard to come by. Learning to read was a dear, yet elusive dream for many, including the poor farm boy Gao Yubao, for example. Many were deprived of learning and reading because of poverty and oppression.

Nowadays, poverty is a thing of the past for most and no one can bar people from reading. Yet our hectic life has become an obstacle and many agonize over never having the time or leisure to read.

Well, the real problem is there are too many temptations.

Reading is unlike an aromatic stress treatment; probably not as appealing as a sumptuous dinner. Reading is altogether a solitary undertaking, far removed from the tantalizing ruckus of wining and dining. Reading forces you to pause and ponder; definitely not an uproarious joyride. Reading may even bring out a deeply felt pain and a tumult of emotions, with a dose of repentance and self-discovery.

Yet, a great read is a powerful, life-giving experience, for as you read, you are traversing the world with the finest minds that have been there before, and you are not trudging alone.

改变在电光石火间

本书，就是一群念头的菜园子。作者只是种菜的老农，把自家的西红柿、萝卜种出来之后，便不知它们将走向何方，有何际遇。而那些念头走街串巷，深入千家万户，走得更远。它们是一个个陌生人，却能很轻易地走进许多人的心灵。

因此，我相信，一定有一本书，藏在远方。它是我们的至交，它的肚腹中藏着一句话，有可能改变我们精神世界的架构，进而影响我们的行为方式，最后甚至扭转我们的人生轨迹。

为什么看似单薄甚至不堪一击的书本，却在

某种程度上很容易改变我们呢？因为，你不是作者，对书没有戒心。

在接受理念的时候，太尊敬和太叛逆，都不是好事。太尊敬了，就隔着一道天堑，觉得彼此的境况可比性太差，适用于你的不应适用于我，甚至是肯定不适用于我，于是被尊敬引到另外的岔道上。至于太叛逆的时候，那是谁的话都听不进去，灵魂的抽屉已塞得满满，没有空隙再放入一张A4纸。当我们漫不经心的时候，所有的警戒都已放下，懒散着，安全地翻着书页，润物细无声的改变反倒容易发生。

人在放松的时候，潜意识就像池塘里的小鱼，快乐地游动起来。而人们的绝大部分生活正是受着潜意识的控制，潜意识有时比我们的意识还要健康。它善良、聪敏、不墨守成规、不故步自封，甚至也不自卑。它更能分辨什么是对这具躯体有用、有好处的东西。

当你和书交流时，你就是放松的。当书中的某一句话，在不经意之间和你的潜意识发生轻轻碰撞的当儿，有一些很重要的你未曾意识到的改变，就在电光石火中产生了。

Change Happens in an Instant

A book is a garden of ideas; its author the gardener. The fruits and greens from the garden disperse; joy to the eye, delighting the palate of many, unbeknownst to the gardener. A book goes further afield; traversing the country like a troubadour and getting through to those who behold it.

There is a book special to each of us, so I like to think, waiting to be found by us. It will be a loyal friend who will be there for us always. A single line in its pages may have the power to change our spiritual foundation, impact how we live, and alter our life's trajectory forever.

Why do books, seemingly insubstantial and brittle,

somehow have the power to easily change us? The answer lies in the fact that when you open a book, you are not the author, but an unguarded reader.

As a reader, you should be wary of being either too reverent or too stubborn. Reverence hampers understanding; a chasm between the reader and new ideas. Absolutely awe-struck, you think the author's experience is neither terribly relevant nor applicable to you. Being too stubborn, you resist any input; a closed mind, like a drawer chock-full of junk having no spare room for even a single sheet of paper. Only when we leave our apprehension at the door, feeling relaxed and safe in the company of a book, flipping through its pages at leisure, do we begin to sense that something magical is quietly happening.

When we are relaxed, our subconscious mind awakens, quick as a darting minnow in a pond. The subconscious mind, in fact, influences much of a person's life. Its positive effect on our wellbeing sometimes outweighs that of the conscious mind. Its power can be innately good, quick and penetrating, uninhibited, liberating, and self-assured. It is susceptible to all that is good and beneficial, to our physique and psyche.

When you are in dialogue with a book, you are at ease. When a sentence inadvertently strikes a chord in your subconscious mind, a change, unbeknownst to you, may be set in motion; with force akin to lightning.

风的青睐

四百年前的法国人蒙田，说过这样一句话——风不会对漫无目标者有所青睐。"青睐"是指一个人用黑眼珠子看着你。这是一个否定句，意思是假如你有了坚定的目标，整个大自然将帮助你。

风是什么呢？风是一股看不见摸不着的力量。风吹的时候，影响着我们，逆风或是顺风，对我们的速度和方向都有强烈的影响。就连飞机的钢铁巨翅，也不敢对风等闲视之。

人生的目标很重要。这个目标是谁给我们预定的呢？没有人。你的父母、你的师长、你的朋友，都可能参与你的目标的制定，但他们不是决定的力量。最后的赞成或是否决票，在你手里。如果你对自己说，我才不要什么人生的目标这种奇怪的东西，那么，你也是有一个目标了，那就是"虚无"。

一个没有方向感的人，如何行走呢？看看醉汉就明白了。踉踉跄跄、东倒西歪、昏乱嘟囔着，没有人知道他要到哪里去，更不知道他的归宿在何方……有着这种精神的罗姆人，终身流浪在灵魂的荒原。

还有一些人，把某种流行的腐朽说法或是误区当成了自己的目标。这种"镜花水月"的伪目标，只能引诱感官的堕落和本能的麻痹。

目标通常是阔大的、依稀的，但它确实存在着，一如晨曦。你从未摸到晨曦，但你每天都可以看到它。即使乌云蔽日的时候，你也坚忍不拔地确信，在高远之处，晨曦依然发出温暖的红色光芒。

一个有目标的人，走路的姿势是向前的。他们通常不会在跌倒之后太长久地抚摸伤痛，短暂的昏厥之后迅速清醒，用身边的树枝或是草叶捆扎好伤口，就蹒跚着上路了。他们走得慢，但很坚定，不会因为风险而避开既定的方向，也不会为路边一些小的花果而长时间地流连忘返。当然也有痴迷和混沌的时候，但他们能够重新恢复思考，从容向前……

　　风的青睐，是无价的礼物。只要你坚定地确立了自己的目标，努力下去，就会发现天地万物都来帮你了。

Fortune Smiles on the Purposeful

Four centuries ago, the Frenchman Michel de Montaigne said, "No wind favours he who has no destined port." It follows from this double negative one-liner that we will be blessed by providence if we are purposeful.

What then is meant by "wind?" It is the force, invisible and intractable, that can impact on the speed and direction of our progress. We may have a headwind, or wind at our back. Either way, we risk peril if we overlook their importance. The same holds true for the flying machine with gigantic metal wings.

It is important to have a life purpose. Yet, who else, other than yourself, can name your destined port? No one. Not even your parents, mentors or friends, who may give you advice but not decide your destination. You alone will cast the ultimate vote. If you say to yourself that you want nothing to do with this "purpose of life" nonsense, then you have named your purpose — to be purposeless.

How does an aimless person proceed in life? You need look no further than the drunken reveller, lumbering, wobbling and mumbling. No one knows where he is headed or will end up. The vagabond, too, wander from one spiritually desolate place to the next.

Still others may come under the influence of decadent, nihilistic ideas, which drive them to pursue hedonistic gratifications, to the point of wanton numbness.

Your purpose can be all-encompassing, evocative, yet real, like the first glow of dawn. You never actually touch it, yet it is there on the horizon, even when clouds blocked the sun; for you believe unflinchingly that behind the clouds, high in the atmosphere, is the radiant glow.

The purposeful lean into the wind and recover quickly from setbacks, rather than grieve and lick their wounds forever. After a bad fall or some hard knocks, they patch themselves up like a hardy warrior, with vines and leaves if need be, and move on. They may start slow, even with a limp, yet are never short of resolve. They do not stray from their chosen path merely to skirt a risk, nor dally and be distracted by temptations along the way. They may have moments of doubt and confusion, yet regain their presence of mind after reorientation, assuredly carrying on...

Then they have the wind at their back; what a blessing! So long as you have a firm, clearly defined goal, and never stop doing your best, you will soon find fortune smiles on you, too.

每只小狗都有一个目标

有一对夫妇有两个孩子，一个叫莎拉，一个叫克里斯汀。当孩子还小的时候，父母决定为他们养一只小狗。小狗抱回来以后，他们想请一位朋友帮忙训练这只小狗。他们搂着小狗来到朋友家，安然坐下。在第一次训练前，女驯狗师问，小狗的目标是什么？夫妻俩面面相觑，很是意外，他们实在想不出狗还有什么另外的目标，嘟囔着说，一只小狗的目标？那当然就是当一只狗了。女驯狗师极为严肃地摇了摇头说，每只小狗都得有一个目标。

夫妇俩商量之后，为小狗确立了一个目标——

白天和孩子们一道玩，夜里要能看家。后来，小狗被成功地训练成了孩子的好朋友和家中财产的守护神。

这对夫妇就是美国的前任副总统阿尔·戈尔和他的妻子迪帕。他们牢牢地记住了这句话——做一只狗要有目标。推而广之，做一个人也要有目标。

在现实生活中，却有太多太多的人没有目标。其实寻找目标并不是一件太难的事，关键是你要知道天下有这样一件唯此唯大的事，然后尽早来做。正是你自己需要一个目标，而不是你的父母或是你的老师或是你的上级需要它。它的存在，和别人的关系都没有和你的关系那样密切。也就是说，它将是你最亲爱的伙伴，其血肉相连的程度，绝对超过了你和你的父母，你和你的妻子儿女，你和你的同伴及领导的关系。你可能丧失了所有的财产和所有的亲人，但只要你的目标还在，你就还有一个完整的系统存在，你就并不孤独和无望。

我们常常把别人的期待当成了自己的目标，在孩童的时候，这几乎是顺理成章的事情。但是，你会渐渐地长大，无论别人的期望是怎样的美好，它也不属于你。除非有一天，你成功地在自己的心底移植了这个期望，这个期望生根发芽，长成了你的目标。那时，尽管所有的枝叶都和原本的母本一脉相承，但其实它已面目全非，它的灵魂完完全全只属于你，它被你的血脉所濡养。

我们常常把世俗的流转当成自己的目标。这一阵子崇尚钱，你就把挣钱当成了自己的目标。殊不知钱只是手段而非目标，有了钱之后，事情远远没有结束。把钱当成目标，就是把叶子当成了根。目标是终极的代名词，它悬挂在人生的瀚海之中，你向它航行，却永远不会抵达。你的快乐就在这跋涉的过程中流淌，而并非把目标攫为己有。从这个意义上说，钱不具备终极目标的资格。过一阵子流行美丽，你就把制造美丽保存美丽当成了目标。殊不知美丽的标准有所不同，美丽是可以变化的，目标却是相当恒定的。美丽之后你还要做什么？美丽会褪色，目标却永远鲜艳。

有人把快乐和幸福当成了终极目标，这也值得推敲。快乐并不只是单纯的快感，类乎饮食和繁殖的本能。科学家们通过研究，发现最长远最持久的快乐，来自你的自我价值的体现。而毫无疑问，自我价值是从属于你的目标感，一个连目标都没有的人，何谈价值呢！

一棵树的目标也许是雕成大厦的栋梁，也许是撑一把绿伞送人阴凉儿，也许是化作无数张白纸传递知识，也许是制成筷子让人大快朵颐……还有数不清的可能性，我们不是树，我们不可能穷尽也不可能明白树的心思。我们是人，我们可以为自己确立一个目标，这是做人的本分之一。

Each Puppy Needs a Purpose

A couple, having bought a puppy for their two little daughters, Sarah and Kristin, sought help from a friend to train the puppy. With the puppy in their arms, they went over to the friend's place. As they were seated, the trainer's first question, before the session got going, was: "What is this puppy's purpose?" Exchanging bewildered looks, the couple mumbled, "Purpose? Er, to be a dog, of course." They couldn't think of any other answer to this unexpected question. With a serious look, the dog trainer shook her head and said, "Each puppy needs a purpose."

The couple decided, after a quick discussion, its purpose

would be for the children to play with during the day and a watch dog at night. The puppy was successfully trained, becoming a great pal for the children and a sentinel for the home.

The couple are the former U.S. Vice President Al Gore and his wife Tipper. They took the dog trainer's advice to heart — Puppies Must Have a Purpose, and, by extension, every human being, like puppies, must also have a well-defined purpose.

Far too many live their lives purposelessly. Yet, finding one's purpose in life is not something impossible. You must first be keenly aware that it is important and imperative, and should be done early in life. It is in fact an intrinsic need of your own, rather than that of your parents, teachers or superiors. Your purpose is something you believe in deeply and is dear to you; nothing and no one else even come close — not even your parents, spouse, offspring, old chums or superiors. You may lose everything — your possessions and your loved ones; yet as long as you have purpose, you have a scheme of meaning — your reason of being. You are beyond solitude and despair.

We often mistook the expectations of others for our purpose. It may have seemed natural when you were little. Yet you grow out of them over time, and other people's expectations, however inspiring, are really not your own. You may internalize such expectations, letting them become seeds of hope and grow into a purpose. Then, they are no longer the same, they become something of your own; your identity, your soul.

Consumed by the changing fads of our society, we often adopt them as our purpose. When money-centrism gains wide currency, making more money becomes a goal in life. Yet money is but a means to an end. If you let making money be your goal in life, you are putting the cart before the horse. When you are rolling in dough, the story doesn't end there. Our purpose should be something akin to the ultimate concern, which forever inspires us to strive and press on. It is not a port we reach at the voyage's end; it is the voyage itself, spanning the entirety of our existential life. In striving to live a life of purpose, we derive endless joy. The pursuit of money is not in the same league at all. The same is true for the fad exalting beauty. While its criteria shift and beauty changes, our purpose in life endures. What happens when you have beauty galore? Beauty fades; purpose remains intense.

Some set the pursuit of joy and happiness as their ultimate goal, which is also debatable. Scientists have found that the most enduring and lasting joy comes from self-actualization, rather than hedonistic gratifications and sensory pleasures derived from food and procreation. Purpose concerns self-worth. There is no worth to speak of for a man without a life purpose.

A tree may have a purpose in being a beam or pillar in a towering building, the pole of an umbrella providing shade in the scorching sun, or reams of paper for the spread of knowledge, or chopsticks for the enjoyment of sumptuous food, or countless other possibilities, which we have no way of exhausting. We are not trees and know not their intentions. Yet, as humans, we should all have a purpose in life; it is one of the things we do that define our humanity.

决定日月，决定悲喜

别听信那些说年轻有多么美好的话，听了也千万不要当真。

青春时，你一无所有，有的只是特别敏感的神经和特别匮乏的机遇。当然，还有双手和大脑。

不要津津乐道那些贵人相助云开雾散的故事。那是极小概率的事件，而你，不过是大概率当中的一员。养成自甘普通的心态非常重要，可以让你一辈子宠辱不惊。有道是由俭入奢易，由奢入俭难。认定自己是普通人，就是情绪上的勤俭持家。偶遇常人难以企及的好运，就是人生的奢侈。不用怕自己适应不了天降祥瑞，就提前天天一厢情愿地预演美事。白日梦做多了，容易怨天尤人走火入魔。

不要对比，滋生沮丧。人和人是不一样的。比父母，你如处在低等阶层，就会生出父母不如人的怨气。而我们永远不能怨恨父母将我们生出，生命神圣。比相貌，假如你不是国色天香潘安再世，就会生出自卑心理。相貌是不可改变的，你必须接受天然的模样，从此泰然处之。比学历，假如你不够高，你可以继续努力读书。假如你所热爱的事务，主要需从实践中学习，那你就不必拘泥于一纸文书，你可以努力让自己成为这一行的佼佼者，再去教导后人。比房子大小，更是和动物撒尿圈领地属于同等级别，没有意思的事情。你知道史上那些英雄豪杰住过的房子是多少平方米吗？如果你不知道，那就证明这件事不能青史留名。也许你说你是普通人，那就更没有必要在这件事情上攀比了。从环保的角度讲，人不应该霸占那么大的地方，留给别人更多的空间，是一种修养。

年轻人常常感觉很无助，无助的根源就在于比较。只要你收起了比较，你就享得了最基本的自由。

年轻时神经非常敏锐，感官非常丰富。一切痛苦都会被放大，令你哀痛难熬。一切欢乐又那么稍纵即逝，令你惆怅惋惜。你常常以为，当你拥有了某些东西，比如业绩，比如融进一个城市，比如住在豪宅，比如提升到某个职务，比如获得了某个奖励，比如娶了美女或是嫁了高富帅——从此你就掉到蜜罐里永无痛楚。但真实的情况是，你拥有了那些东西之后，忧愁依然在，茫然依然在，唯一不在的是你的耐心。

我看过一个资料，说是这世界上真正有作为的专家，要对所操行业达到专精，至少要经过一万个小时以上的学习或是训练。关于天赋和师资等条件咱们姑且不论，单是时间，就漫长到绝望。按每日五小时浸淫其中（专注的时间太长，反倒没有效率。此处指的是全神贯注的高质量学习），要两千天。按照每年两百个工作日计算，需要整整十年。

十年！足以让一个血气方刚的青年，变成沉着稳健的中年。

年轻时磨炼之意义，就在于因为这过程你经历过，就在于你终于知道它的转归。你必须有耐心，在看起来毫无希望的时候，不急于求成。举个自己的例子，很多我年轻时在意的东西，现在已经褪去颜色。我在意过生死，当我距离它尚远的时候，噤若寒蝉。当我离它更近的时候，反倒从容。我在意过名次，现在索性不参加比赛了。怡然耕耘的人，汗水之外，两袖清风。我在意过朋友的多寡，现在才知道，有一些人当初就不是为了友谊而来。如落叶遇到风霜，散去本是正常。不变的是我的人生，越来越静谧。

年轻时多选择，每个选择都通往不同的道路，每逢选择时就会不安，生怕一着不慎，满盘皆输。比如，在街头一间不算太大的超市里，共有超过两万五千多种商品可供你选择。只要你乐意购买，有将近一万份杂志和期刊可供你阅读。你还可以选择收看几百个电视台的任何一个频道。更不用说打开电脑，有海量的信息如原始时期的大洪水扑来，可以将你淹得两眼翻白。

不用那么紧张。

只要你的选择和你的人生大方向相一致，你的基本价值观是真善美的，那么，就不会犯原则性的错误。这就是年轻的好处，走错了，你可以重新再来。如果因为怕犯错误而驻足不前，那才是枉费了青春，犯了最大的错误。

年轻的时候，你除了可以决定自己的方向和选择之外，再就是可以决定心情。你会没有很多东西，但你一定有自己的心情。你不能改变很多东西，但你一定能改变自己的心情。所以，你可以决定日月，决定悲喜。

你或许要说，日和月，多么光芒万丈的天体，我哪里就能决定它们呢？别着急，日和月合在一起，是什么？是明天的"明"字啊。通过努力，我们可以把握自己的明天，让自己开始喜悦的早晨。

Your Mood, Your Day

Never believe those who say youth is all beautiful; a field of dreams. It is a claim not to be taken for real. You have little to your name when you are young, save edgy nerves and woefully few opportunities. Then, of course, your hands and brain.

Quit soaking up tales of blissful patronage, too, for the probability of its happening to you is next to null. You are one in a million — the multitudes who are not favoured by any expeditious benefaction. So, it is very important to be content with being ordinary. Then you are unruffled by either honour or humiliation. We take it in stride when our circumstances improve, but not the other way round. Recognizing we are but run-of-the-mill, we attain an emotional equilibrium, knowing good fortune being a rare luxury and never a given in life. We should stop dreaming endlessly about any unlikely god-send to the point of make-believe, for it will only lead us astray and reduce us to grudging souls when our dream fails to come true.

Stop comparing yourself to others, for it is demoralizing. We are all different. When you compare yourself with those with parents on a higher social perch, such comparisons only make you sulky and resentful. Yet life is sacred. How can we grudge our parents who have given us life? When you compare yourself to someone prettier, you are made to feel inferior. We cannot change our looks; we have to accept and content ourselves with what we have. Why compare?

Of course, if you think your qualifications are

not as good as others', you can take a course. If what you are passionate about is learned mostly through practice, you can learn while doing it. With hard work, you will excel in your chosen field, without having a fancy degree or diploma, and then help others to learn as well. It's also senseless to compare who has the larger dwelling, which is not much different from beasts' urine-marking. Nobody remembers the floor space, in square meters or any other measure, that the great and heroic in human history occupied for their dwelling. Such things never go down in history. You may say you are no heroes. Then, it makes even less sense to compare. Besides, a small footprint and leaving room for fellow humans is not only environmentally sound, but also a mark of cultivation.

Comparison is at the root of the powerlessness often felt by young people. If you stop comparing, you will feel a liberating sense of freedom.

When you are young, you are delicately sensitive and keenly observant. Your feelings of pain are often magnified to the point of being excruciating and unbearable, while joy fleeting; leaving you by and large in a perpetual state of melancholy and poignant regret. You may have imagined that once you have achieved what you desire — stellar performance at work, settling into life in the city, a posh apartment, a top job, a plump bonus, marrying a pretty sweetheart or rich, handsome heartthrob — you'd trot off being happy and contented forever. The truth is you won't. You'd still feel forlorn and lost as before. But you'd have no patience anymore.

I once read that it takes at least 10,000 hours of study or practice to truly become an expert at just about anything. It's a lot of time; long enough to drive people to despair, not to mention the buckets of talent and the good mentor that you will need. At an average of five hours per day (of fully attentive quality work; longer than that, your effectiveness begins to slide), it will come to 2,000 days, or ten full years at 200 working days per year.

Ten years! Enough for someone in the bloom of youth to mellow into middle age.

You go through trials and tribulations in youth to gain experience and appreciate that things change. You must have patience; bide your time when success seems beyond reach. For me, a lot that I cared about back in my time no longer invokes the same emotions. I used to ponder on death a lot, which haunted me, sending chills down my spine, when it was but a remote prospect. Now that I have come nearer, it haunts me no more. I cared about winning. Now I decline all competitions; content to live by the sweat of my brow, and unfettered by worldly temptations. I cared about having or losing friends. I know now not all who hang around are there for friendship. Some fade away, as leaves scatter after the first frost. What's constant is life — that of mine; ever more tranquil and unfettered now.

Life is full of choices when we are young; each leads to a different path. When it is time for a decision, we become anxious, fearful that a misstep might ruin all our chances. We are overwhelmed by options. In any supermarket of a regular size, there can be over 25,000 different kinds of merchandize. If you care to browse, there are nearly 10,000 magazine tiles published in China. As for the digital media, there are hundreds of television channels to choose from, not to mention all the online sources of information, accessible at a few keyboard clicks. With the torrential flow of data, you are up to your eyeballs.

Fret not. If you are guided by your calling in life, with the values of truth, goodness and beauty as your compass, you will not err on matters of principle. You can always start again after a misstep — that's the great thing about being young. What a crime it would be to waste youth in inaction for fear of making errors!

Being young, you have the power to choose your mood, in addition to your path forward. You may have few possessions to speak of. Yet you are the master of your own moods. You may not yet be able to change a lot of things, but you surely have your mood at your command and you can determine how your days and months will be.

— Well, how can I determine days and months? It has to be those celestial bodies, the sun and the moon, you may retort.

Yet, in the Chinese script, the sun and day are represented by the same ideogram (日), and the moon and month, the ideogram (月). Both, when combined, form the composite ideogram tomorrow (明) — future. As you determine how your days and months should be, as you begin your day with verve and joy, you can, through your own efforts, shape your future.

所有的动力都来自内心的沸腾

一个人躺在地上，如果他不想起来，那么十个人也拉不起他来，即使起来了也马上会趴下。所有的动力都来自内心的沸腾。如果你做不到一件事，无论是搞好关系，寻找爱人，还是减肥，都是因为你还没有真正想做。

这是一个很有意思的心理小游戏。来，纠集起十来个人，然后找一个人来扮演那个躺在地上的人，不用找体重特别沉的，那样容易影响咱们这个游戏的真实感。请这位朋友赖在地上，大家用尽全力把他拽起来……

我见过三十来个人都拉不起一个人的，我本来在上文中想写这个数字，但又怕人家觉得太夸张了，就写了十来个人，这是千真万确的。只要你不想起来，没有人能把你拉起来。心理上的问题也是一样，只要你没有想通，只要你不是真的心服口服，那么所有外界的努力都是劳而无功的。

　　女子当了妈妈，对待自己的孩子时，要记得这个游戏。他虽然小，也有自己的独立意志，你要把道理给他讲清楚，而且要让他明白这样做的目的是什么，有人会觉得孩子还小，没必要讲那么多。可是，成长是一个逐渐发生的过程，你不能在一颗幼小的心里，种下强权的种子，以理服人而不是以力服人，这是要从小就养成的习惯。

　　你举目四望，很容易就能发现：很多人的生理上的需求得到了满足，但他们仍然不满意，奔突不止，躁动不安，缺少一种能使他变得生机勃勃的动力，缺乏稳定祥和。像这样缺乏主动性的生活，无论表面上多么风光，都是不值得羡慕的。

　　那种使自己变得生机勃勃的动力是什么呢？谁来回答你呢？谁来帮你寻找呢？谁为你一锤定音呢？没有别人，只有你自己。

　　只有当理想的光芒照耀着我们，而且它和广大人群的福祉相连，我们才会有大的安宁和勇气。

　　你可曾体会种子的疼痛？那种挣开包裹自己的硬壳，顶出板结的土壤的苦难，对一粒柔弱的芽来说，可说是顶天立地的壮举。一个人觉醒时的力量，应该大于一颗种子啊！

有些人把梦想变成现实，有些人把现实变成了梦想。关键是，你的梦想是什么？你为你的梦想做了什么？

有梦想就不会寂寞，当你寂寞的时候，只要招招手，你的梦想就飞到了身边。剩下的事，就是琢磨怎样把梦想变成行动了。

Power from Within

It is a hell of an effort to get someone off the floor, if he is unwilling. Not even when you have ten people helping to pull him up. He'd slump the moment you let go. Drive comes from within. You will fail to achieve anything, be it getting along with others, finding a romantic partner or getting into shape, if your spirit is unwilling.

It is an interesting game of willpower. Gather a dozen people and name the one who is to lie on the floor. He needn't be particularly heavy, which may spoil the game. With the person squarely on the floor, the rest of the group are to try their best to pull him up...

I have seen thirty people trying and failing. I mentioned ten at the outset only because I feared that thirty may sound incredulous. But I wasn't exaggerating. As long as you are unwilling, no one can get you off the ground. The same goes for psychological problems. Efforts by others will come to naught, unless you yourself think things through and be totally convinced.

If you are a mother, please remember the morale of this little game when dealing with your children. You need to clearly explain why you want them to do things in a certain way, for they have their own autonomous will, even though they are little. Some may think it unnecessary since they are so young. Yet, you should never force your ideas on them, which would instil fear of coercion in them. Help them acquire the habit, when they are young, of using reason, not force in dealing with others, by showing them your example.

You may often see discontented souls who have all the creature comforts they want, yct are perennially fretful and ill at ease. They lack the drive that may make them full of vigour and self-assured. Their life, lacking intrinsic energy and peace, is nothing to be admired of, not matter how glamorous it may look on the outside.

What is the intrinsic force, the source of vigour? Who can give or help you find the answer? Who holds the key? It is none other than you.

Only when we are driven by aspirations that are in sync with the wellbeing of humanity will we find profound inner peace and courage.

Have you ever imagined the painful awakening of a seed, breaking through its own husk and the hardened crust of soil? It must have been a tremendous struggle for something as feeble as a tiny seed. The awakening of an individual can only be even more so!

Some live their dream while others live in their dream. The crux of the matter is how you define your dream and what you do to make it come true.

Those with aspirations will not be plagued by emptiness. All they need to do is think how best to turn aspirations into real actions.

别给人生留遗憾

关于"遗憾"，我查过字典，字典里有各式各样的解释，我最喜欢的一个解释就是——能够去满足的心愿，可是我们没有去完成，深感惋惜。我想跟大家说的，是在我年轻的时候，让我感到万分遗憾的事情，那件事情如果发生了，我今天根本就不可能站在这里和大家做这样的一番分享。

一九六九年的时候，我不到十七岁，就穿上军装从北京出发到达新疆。我们坐上了大卡车，经过六天的奔波，翻越天山，到达了新疆的喀什。我的战友们都留在了那里，我们五个女兵又继续，坐上大卡车向藏北出发了。这一次，这个世界在我的面前，已经不是平坦的了，它好像完全变成了一个竖起来的世界，每一天的海拔都在升高，从三千米到四千米，从四千米到五千米，直到最后，翻越了六千米的界山达坂，它是新疆和西藏分界的一个山脉。进入了西藏阿里，我恍惚觉得这已经不再是地球了，它荒凉的程度，让我怀疑这是不是火星或者是月亮的背面。

我记得一九七一年的时候，我们要去野营拉练，时间正处寒冬腊月。我们要背着行李包，要背着红十字箱，要背上手枪，要背上手榴弹，还有几天的干粮，一共是六十斤重。高原之上，寒冬腊月，滴水成冰，当时的温度已经是零下四十摄氏度，有一天早上三点钟就吹起了起床号，说我们今天要翻越无人区，无人区一共有一百二十里的路，中间不可以有任何的停留，要一鼓作气地走过去，因为那里条件特别恶劣，而且没有水。

走啊走啊走啊走啊，走到下午两三点的时候吧，我觉得那个十字背包袋，已经全部嵌入到我的锁骨里面去了，我觉得喉头不断地在发咸发苦，一句话都说不出来，我想我要吐一口肯定是血，我想这样的苦难何时才能结束呢，我想我年轻的生命，为什么我所有的神经末梢，都用来忍受这种非人的痛苦。我当时就做了一个决定，今天此刻我一定要自杀，不活了，面对的这种苦难无法忍受。这样决定了以后，我就开始打算什么时间坠崖而亡。

就这样不断地在找合适的地点，不断地在找合适的时机，终于我找到了一个特别适合的地方，往上看是峭壁高耸，往下看是深不见底的悬崖，我想我只要松下手掉下去，我一定会死。但是在最后一刹那，我突然发现我后面的那个战友，他离得我太近了，我如果下去的话，一定会把他也带到悬崖之下，我在想我已经决定要死，可是我不应该拖累了别人。队伍在行进中，这样的好时机也是稍纵即逝，之后地势又变得比较平坦，我再想找这么一个地方，就不容易了。

这样走着走着天黑了，我们走到了目的地。一百二十里路就这样走过去了，那六十斤的负重，也一两都不少地被我背到了目的地。我站在那片雪原之上，把自己的全身都摸了一遍，每一个指关节，膝盖，包括我的双脚。我确信在经历了这样的苦难之后，我的身体连一根头发都没有少。那一天给了我一个特别深刻的教育，那就是当我们常常以为自己顶不住的时候，并不是最后的时刻，而是我们的精神崩溃之时。而你只要重整精神，整理心情，再次出发，哪怕是万劫不复，也依然可以去找到它的出口，也依然可以坚持下去。

我了解年轻的朋友们，也知道在我们的生活当中，会有各式各样的苦难。有时候有的家长跟我说，您能告诉我一个方法吗，让我的孩子少受苦难？我说，我能告诉你的，唯一可以确定的事情是，你的孩子必然遭受苦难。我们年轻的时候，我们的神经是那么敏感，我们的记忆是那么清晰，我们的感情是那么充沛，我们每一道伤都会流出热血。所以尽管有很多人告诉你们，年轻时是一个人最美好的时候，我也想告诉你们，年轻也是我们痛苦的时候，我们会留下很多很多的遗憾。那么最大的遗憾，就是断然结束自己的生命，我想这是对生命的大不敬。而且以我个人的经历来讲，那一天我没有结束自己的生命，我坚持下来了，我才发现，原来那最不可战胜的，并不是我们的遭遇，而是我们内心的坚强。

　　日本有一位医生，他的工作就是专门去照顾那些临终的病人。他和大约一千名临终的病人谈过以后，总结出了二十五条人生的遗憾，其中包括：没有吃到美食，没有回过自己的故乡，自己的孩子没有结婚，等等。

　　我和这位医生也深有同感，因为我曾经去过临终关怀医院，也陪伴着那些临终的人，走向他们生命的最后时刻，也跟他们有过很多倾心的交谈。我曾经到一间临终者的病房，那儿住着一位八十岁的老人，连他的儿女们都不再陪伴在他的身边了。他的儿女们都在外面，说他们不忍心看到那最后一刻，我说那我愿意进去陪伴他。我走进那个房间，深深地吸了一口气。我觉得在这个空气里有很多很多临终病人最后吐出的气息。然后我躺在那位老人的身边，摸着他的手，那个老人轻轻地跟我说了一句话，他说，我觉得我这一辈子，怎么好像没活过啊。

我今天把这个故事和年轻的朋友们来分享，是想说：

我们每一个人的生命都是一张单程的火车票，我们每一个人都没有拿到返程的那张票。所以生命从我们出生那天开始，它就像箭一样地射向远方，我们能够在自己手里，把持住的就是我们此时此刻，这无比宝贵的生命。

我特别想说，我希望我们的理想服从于我们的价值观。在我们的心里，能够燃烧起熊熊火焰的，并且给我们的一生以指引和动力的，是我们对于自己认为最美好的那些价值的追求。

举个我个人的小例子，二〇〇八年的时候，我终于用我的稿费，买了一张船票开始去环球旅行。走啊走啊，走了没多远，才走到中国南海，就发生了汶川地震。船上有一千多个外国客人，只有六个中国人，可是我说，我们一定要为中国发起一场募捐。后来我们的团队里有人就说，那些外国人要是不给咱们捐钱，我们多么丢脸呐。我说，可是我们中国人要不为自个儿的祖国做点什么，那才是丢脸呢。我们说我们一定只募捐美元和欧元，这样的话，会让我们那个（捐款）数字变大，如果我们募捐人民币，人家会觉得只有我们自己捐。我们自己先捐出了美元和欧元，但是当募捐结束，所有的钱都揽到一起的时候，船长对我说，里面有两千元人民币。

只有我们六个中国人，是谁捐的人民币，这很容易查呀。吃饭的时候，我们就互相问，谁捐的人民币？我们不是说了要捐美元和欧元吗？最后我们六个人都说没有捐人民币。后来我就跟船长说，这船上除我们以外还有中国人吗？船长说在深不见底的底舱有，不过他们永远不能到甲板上来的，那些工人里有你们中国人。我回到北京就把这个钱捐了，北川中学知道我回国了就打来电话，说希望我到北川中学，去当一次语文老师，因为我有一篇小散文，叫作《提醒幸福》，收在全国统编教材初中二年级的课本里。

我不怕地震，可是我有点怕，我写的这篇文章的题目，它叫《提醒幸福》。那样的大震之后，他们的老师有伤亡，他们的同学有很多很多再也不能回到教室里。我觉得在这种困难的情况下，让我去跟他们讲"提醒幸福"，幸福在哪里？但是那一次北川中学之行，给予了我巨大的震撼。因为北川中学初中二年级，所有的同学聚在一起，他们告诉我说，他们是世界上最幸福的人。我说，你们说自己是最幸福的人，你能告诉我你们幸福在哪里吗？后来他们告诉我说，那么多人死了我们还活着，这就是幸福。

"我们在马路上看到，全中国所有省份的汽车都来了，我们就觉得全国人民在帮助我们；大震才过去了十几天，我们今天就可以恢复读书了……难道我们还不是世界上最幸福的人吗！"我听了以后真的热泪盈眶，我才知道在生死面前，最宝贵的东西是什么，在重新享有生命的时候，一定要把自己价值观中，那些最重要的东西放在前面。

我下个月会出发到非洲去，我以前觉得那是我的一个愿望，但是如果我不抓紧去实现它的话，我会越来越老，身体也会慢慢地有更多的问题：也许我的眼睛不再那样明亮，看不了非洲的动物；也许我的思维不再那么敏捷，对于非洲灿烂的文化和悠远的历史，理解起来，回忆起来，可能就会有困难。我可能还要翻山越岭，万一自己跑不动被狮子追上了，是不是也有点危险？

所以如果你有愿望，如果你真的还有力量去实行它，我觉得一定要即刻就出发，去完成自己的愿望，减少自己的遗憾。人生是一个漫长的过程，年轻是多么的美好，但是请你们记得：记得有很多的东西，当你不懂的时候，你年轻，当你懂得了以后，你已年老。

那么让我们的理想不要变成化石，让我们现在就行动起来，去实践我们的理想，让我们的人生少些遗憾。

Let There Be Fewer Regrets

Of all the definitions for the word regret I found in dictionaries, here is the one I liked the most — a deep sense of dissatisfaction over not achieving a desired end once within reach.

What I'd like to share with you is an experience of mine from years ago. Should the event on that fateful day have happened, my young life would have been a huge disappointment. I wouldn't even be standing here and having this dialogue with you today.

It was 1969 and I had just joined the army before turning seventeen. We left Beijing, all decked out in new army uniforms. Upon our arrival in Xinjiang, we were put on army trucks and began our rumbling, bumpy six-day ride through the Tianshan Mountain, to the town of Kashgar. From there, only five of the female recruits continued on — destination northern Tibet, while the rest of my fellow rookies stayed behind. The flat desert topography ended and the road began a gradual and continuous incline. The land appeared to slant skyward. We gained elevations daily, reaching 4,000, 5,000 meters above sea level..., until we climbed up to the Jieshan Daban pass at an elevation of close to 6,000 meters, across the regional boundary between Xinjiang and Tibet. As the truck trundled into Ngari, the stunning bleakness of the land was such that I began to feel we were as though in some extraterrestrial terrain, Martian or the far side of the moon.

I remember, in the winter of 1971, we were ordered to start a long field march. Each of us carried a load of thirty kilos, which for me included the bedroll, a medic's case, a rifle, hand grenades and rations for several days. It was bitterly cold on the high plateau and water froze instantly upon exposure, as temperature had plummeted to below minus 40 degrees Celsius. One morning, the reveille sounded at three and we were ordered to march 60 kilometres without stop, for there was no water resupply along that stretch of harsh no man's land.

We marched on and on, with no end in sight. By mid-afternoon, the medic's case slung across my shoulder felt so heavy it was cutting into my collarbone. My voice had deserted me. There was a bitter, salty taste in the back of my mouth. It could well be blood had I spat it out. When would this suffering end? I lamented inside. Why should my life, young and barely lived, be subjected to such inhuman torture? I ached all over, with each sensory receptor feeling the excruciating pain. I made a mortal decision — I've had enough, I can't bear any more, I want my life to end right there. With my mind made up, I scanned for a suitable spot and waited for the right time. At last, we came to the edge of a precipice that looked perfect: on one side was the rise of a cliff face and the other a sheer drop into the unfathomable depth. It would be a fall to certain death. However, I realized at that moment a fellow soldier was right behind me. If I had thrown myself off the cliff then, he would most certainly be brought down with me into the abyss. My decision shouldn't cause a collateral death. Then, the momentary window of action slipped away. As we marched on, the land began to flatten. It was hard to find any spot good enough for the purpose.

It grew dark as we approached our destination. The ordeal of the 60K march was over and the 30-kg pack I carried was intact without a single ounce shed. Standing in the snowy wilderness, I gave myself a good pat, knowing with relief the whole of me, too, was intact after the gruelling march; not a single knuckle, toe, knee or hair on my head was damaged or lost. I learned the hard way that it is our mind, not our body that tends to surrender first. If we can harness our brain power and toughen up mentally, we can go on, even though the physical pain becomes abysmal and unbearable.

I know and understand the suffering and hardships, of all descriptions, that my young friends may have faced in their lives. Parents with young children sometimes asked me, "How can my child be spared of suffering?" I would reply, "All I can tell you is suffering is inevitable as your child goes through life." In youth, we are incurably sensitive, our memory keen, our feelings profuse, and our wounds hurt so much. Youth epitomises agony. It is a phase of life that, instead of being beautiful as some might say, leaves you with many regrets. Yet the regret of all regrets is the abrupt ending of our own life. It is blasphemous to the sanctity of life— I had nearly gone there. I didn't end my life that fateful day and endured. I realized that our innate strength and mental toughness are ultimately invincible. It can triumph over physical suffering.

A Japanese doctor who worked in hospice care summed up twenty-five universal regrets in life, after talking with more than one thousand terminally ill patients. They included having not enjoyed a delectable feast, not returned to one's birthplace, or not seen one's offspring getting married.

I had very much the same experiences as the doctor. I, too, spent time with patients at a hospice centre, keeping them company in their last days and hours. I also had many candid, touching conversations with them. I remember an eighty-year-old patient, whose family huddled outside the room, because they couldn't bear seeing the man in his last lingering moments. I told them I would like to be at his bedside. I walked in, taking a deep breath, the air stale with what was exhaled by the terminally ill. I lay beside the octogenarian and gently rubbed his hand, as he murmured, "Why is it I feel I haven't really lived after all…"

By sharing this story with my young friends here today, I meant to say —

Life is a one-way journey. None of us has a return ticket.

From day one, we are propelled forward; each point a point of no return. Seize the day! That is what we have under our control. Each moment of our life and now is precious and beyond compare.

It is my hope, in particular, that our pursuits are driven by our values, those that we believe to be best and noble. They kindle in us an intense, lifelong passion, giving us the moral compass and lasting motivation.

Let me give you a personal example. In 2008, I bought my ticket for a round-the-world cruise, at last with the royalties I earned from my books. It was a long voyage. When we were in the South China Sea after sailing for days, news came that Wenchuan was hit by a major earthquake. There were over a thousand passengers on the cruise ship and only six of us were Chinese. I was determined, "We must organize a donation drive for China." Some in our group were doubtful, saying "How embarrassing it would be if none of the non-Chinese passengers would support us!" "It would be a real shame," I said, "if we don't do something for our own country." It was agreed that we would accept donations only in U.S. dollar or Euro, which would make it an international effort. Otherwise it would look as though only Chinese passengers made donations. Everyone in our group gave in the required currencies. When the drive was concluded, the captain informed me the final tally included 2,000 in Chinese currency.

With only six Chinese passengers on the ship, it wouldn't be too difficult to find out. At the dinnertime, we asked among ourselves, "Didn't we all agree to give U.S. dollars or Euros? Who put in the RMB?" It soon became clear — none of us did. So I went back to the captain, asking, "Are there any other Chinese on the ship?" He told me that among the ship's crew way down blow were some Chinese workers, but they were not allowed to ever come up into the guest areas.

The donations we collected were given to a relief organization upon my return to Beijing. I then got a call from

Beichuan Middle School inviting me to visit and be their Chinese teacher for a day. One of my stories, Celebrate Happiness, had been selected for the national standard textbook for the second year of the middle school.

I was a bit apprehensive, not of the earthquake, but the topic Celebrate Happiness. Some of the school's teachers died or were injured in the calamitous disaster, and many of its students never came back to its classrooms. In light of such, how could I talk about Celebrate Happiness? How could there be any happiness at all? Yet, I was shaken to the core when Year 2 students of the school, who gathered around me during my trip there, told me they were the happiest in the world. I asked, "Can you tell me why? What is your happiness?" Their reply was unanimous, "Because we survived, while so many died."

"When we see in our streets vehicles with

license plates of every province of China, we know the whole nation is behind us. Only a fortnight after the earthquake, we are back in our classrooms... Who can say we are not the most fortunate?" I was touched, my eyes brimming with tears. They who had been to the brink of death taught me instead what is of the greatest value at the edge of life and what should come before all else.

I will take a trip to Africa next month. It has been a long-held wish of mine. I have realized if I don't do it now, I might never do it later, as I am not getting any younger. I will also likely have more health issues — perhaps my eyes will not be as keen, not being able to follow the animals in the African wilderness; my mind not as sharp, not being able to grasp and remember the long history and glory of African civilization. I might even unwittingly fall prey to the roaming king of the jungle, should I fall behind others while trekking in the hills.

Embark on your journey now, if you have the strength and will to realize the wish you have so cherished. Let there be fewer regrets at the end of the road. Life is such a long journey;

youth is indeed wonderful. Yet remember — being young, we are often oblivious, with much beyond our ken; by the time we are sadder and wiser, youth is no more.

So, don't let your dream grow into petrified remains of unfulfilled yearning. Let us take action, to strive and live our dream, here and now. Let there be fewer regrets.

精神的三间小屋

面对那句"人的心灵应该比大地、海洋和天空都更为博大"的名言，人们往往会自惭形秽。我们难以拥有那样雄浑的襟怀。不知累积至那种广袤，需如何积攒每一粒泥土、每一朵浪花、每一朵云霓？

甚至那句恨不能人人皆知的中国古话——宰相肚里能撑船，也让我们在敬仰之余不知所措。也许因为我们不过是小小的草民，即便怀有效仿的渴望，也总是可望而不可即，便以位卑宽宥了自己。

两句关于人的心灵的描述，不约而同地使用了空间的概念。人的肢体活动需要空间。人的心灵活动也需要空间。那容心之所,该有怎样的面积和布置?

人们常常说,安居才能乐业。如今的城里人一见面,就问,你是住两居室还是三居室啊?……喔,两居室窄巴点,三居室虽说并不富余,也算小康了。

身体活动的空间是可以计量的,心灵活动的疆域,是否也有个基本达标的数值?

有一颗大心,才盛得下喜怒,输得出力量。于是,宜选月冷风清、竹木萧萧之处,为自己的精神修建三间小屋。

第一间,盛着我们的爱和恨。对父母的尊爱,对伴侣的情爱,对子女的疼爱,对朋友的关爱,对万物的慈爱,对生命的珍爱……对丑恶的仇恨,对污浊的厌烦,对虚伪的憎恶,对卑劣的蔑视……这些复杂对立的情感,林林总总,会将这间小屋挤得满满的,间不容发。你的一生,经历过的所有悲欢离合、喜怒哀乐,仿佛以木石制作的古老乐器,铺陈在精神小屋的几案上,一任岁月飘逝,在某一个金戈铁马之夜,它们会无师自通,与天地呼应,铮铮作响。假若爱比恨多,小屋就光明温暖,像一座金色池塘,有红色的鲤鱼游弋,那是你的大福气。假如恨比爱多,小屋就凄风苦雨,愁云惨雾,你会精神悲戚压抑,形销骨立。如果想重温祥和,就得净手焚香,洒扫庭院。销毁你的精神垃圾，重塑你的精神天花板，让一束圣洁的阳光，从天窗洒入。

无论一生遭受多少困厄欺诈，请依然相信人类的光明大于暗影。哪怕是只多一个百分点呢，也是希望永恒在前。所以，在布置我们的精神空间时，给爱留下足够的容量。

第二间小屋，盛放我们的事业。

一个人从25岁开始做工，直到60岁退休，要在工作岗位上度过整整35年的时光。按一日工作八小时，一周工作五天计算，每年就要为你的职业付出两千个小时。倘若一直干到退休，那就是七万个小时。在这个庞大的数字面前，相信大多数人都会始于惊骇，终于沉思。假如你所从事的工作，是你的爱好，这七万个小时，将是怎样快活和充满创意的时光！假如你不喜欢它，漫长的七万个小时，足以让花容磨损，日月无光，每一天都如同穿着淋湿的衬衣，针芒在身。

我不晓得一下子就找对了行业的人，能占多大比例。从大多数人谈到工作时乏味麻木的表情推算，估计这样的幸运儿不多。不要轻觑了事业对精神的濡养或反之的腐蚀作用，它以深远的力度和广度，挟持着我们的精神，以成为它麾下持久的人质。

适合你的事业，不靠天赐，主要靠自我寻找。这不但因为相宜的事业，并非像雨后的菌子一样俯拾即是，而且因为我们对自身的认识，也如抽丝剥茧，需要水落石出的流程。你很难预知，将在18岁还是40岁甚至更沧桑的时分，才真正触摸到倾心的爱好。当我们太年轻的时候，因为尚无法真正独立，受种种条件的制约，那附着在事业外壳上的金钱、地位，或是其他显赫的光环，也许会晃了我们的眼。当我们有了足够的定力，将事业之外的赘生物一一剥除，露出它单纯可爱的本质时，可能已耗费半生。然费时弥久，精神的小屋也定须住进你所爱好的事业。否则，鸠占鹊巢，李代桃僵，那屋内必是鸡飞狗跳，不得安宁。

我们的事业，是我们的田野。我们背负着它，播种着，耕耘着，收获着，欣喜地走向生命的远方。规划自己的职业生涯，使事业和人生呈现缤纷和谐、相得益彰的局面，是第二间精神小屋坚固优雅的要诀。

第三间，安放我们自身。

这好像是一个怪异的说法。我们自己的精神住所，不住着自己，又住着谁呢？

可它又确是我们常常犯下的重大失误——在我们的小屋里，住着所有我们认识的人，唯独没有我们自己。我们把自己的头脑变成他人思想汽车驰骋的高速公路，却不给自己的思维留下一条细细的羊肠小道；我们把自己的头脑变成搜罗最新信息和网罗八面来风的集装箱，却不给自己的发现留下一个小小的储藏盒。我们说出的话，无论声音多么嘹亮，都是别的喉咙嘟囔过的；我们发表的意见，无论多么周全，都是别的手指圈画过的。我们把世界万物保管得好好的，偏偏弄丢了开启自己的钥匙，在自己独居的房屋里，找不到自己曾经生存的证据。

如果真是那样，我们的精神小屋，不必等待地震和潮汐，在微风中就悄无声息地坍塌了。它纸糊的墙壁化为灰烬，白雪的顶棚变作泥泞，露水的地面成了沼泽，江米纸的窗棂破裂，露出惨淡而真实的世界。你的精神，孤独地在风雨中飘零。

三间小屋，说大不大，说小不小。在非常世界，建立精神的栖息地，是智慧生灵的义务，每人都有如此的权利。我们可以不美丽，但我们健康。我们可以不伟大，但我们庄严。我们可以不完满，但我们努力。我们可以不永恒，但我们真诚。

当我们把自己的精神小屋建筑得美观结实、储物丰富之后，不妨扩大疆城，增修新舍，矗立我们的精神大厦，开拓我们的精神旷野。因为，精神的宇宙是如此的辽阔啊。

Three Little "Rooms" for Your Soul

We feel humbled by noble largesse, that richness of heart said in that famous adage to "encompass the vastest land, ocean and sky." We find it beyond us, wondering how many miles we must walk, how many waves and clouds we must brave before we can be equal to such mannish munificence.

We feel flummoxed after admiring the forbearance touted in an old Chinese saying known to virtually every man, "A prime minister's heart is too big to take offense." For the man in the street, it is a realm forever out of his reach, however eager he is to emulate. He forgives himself with the easy excuse of his humble station.

Both sayings about the human heart allude to a spatial dimension. We all need space for sheltering our limbs and heart. What dimensions and layout should the space for our heart be?

A family is said to need a stable home to thrive. Nowadays, town folks are thought to be doing well if they own a three-bedroom apartment, a step up, of course, from the somewhat cramped two-bedroom family unit.

The physical space of a home being thus quantified, are there minimum requirements for the space for our soul?"

Our heart should be big enough to hold all our love and hate and to give strength, needing perhaps at least three little "rooms," built with the serenity of a moonlit night and simplicity of an autumnal tree.

The first "room" should be that of love and animus — of reverence for our parents, passion for our partners, affection for our children, camaraderie for our friends, compassion for all creatures great and small and an aching love for life...; of abhorrence of evil, aversion to vice, odium on hypocrisy, loathing of meanness... Such complex, countervailing sentiments can fill up this little "room" to the hilt. All the joys and sorrows in our life, of reunions and inevitable partings, will ascend someday in a wordless song, with soaring notes magically called up, on a momentous night, from ancient musical instruments constructed of wood and jade that have been lying quietly all these years on a side table in the little "room" of our heart.

If the "room" is filled with more love than hate, it takes on a warm glow, like a golden pond with the glimmer of a fish of ruby red gliding in it. And you are truly blessed. Reversely, the "room" will be bleak. You are depressed and despondent; a haggard shadow of yourself. Get rid of the junk cluttering the little "room" with quiet resolve and hard work, so that peace and warmth will return; a ray of sunlight streaming through the skylight.

Keep up your faith in humanity, however

you have suffered or been let down. Light will prevail over darkness. Even if it is by merely one percentage point, there is hope. So, make sure that the first "room" of your heart has enough space for love.

The second "room" is that of work.

A person who starts to work at the age of 25 will have worked 35 years when he retires at 60. That is a total of 70,000 hours, with eight hours a day, five days a week and 2,000 hours each year, to be dedicated to work. At such a colossal figure, most will start to ponder after the initial shock. If your passion is your work, all those hours will be of joy and creativity, or else each will be of toil and trouble, wearing you out and weighing you down.

I do not know the usual percentage of those who find passion in work out of the gate. Judging by the indolent lack of enthusiasm that most show when talking about their work, I figure the blessed souls are few. Never underestimate the effect of our work on our soul, either enriching or corrosive. It can hold our soul hostage endlessly in profound, far-reaching and powerful ways.

Finding one's true calling is never a given. It requires continuous search. It does not crop up like mushrooms after a timely rain, so that all you need to do is reach out and pick one. It is a process of self-discovery and clarification, like peeling back the onion. It is hard to predetermine when you will find your true passion, at 18 or 40, or much later after you have been through trials and tribulations of life. For when we are young, not truly independent and under various constraints, we can be easily distracted, when it comes to career choice, by money, status and other trappings. By the time we are able to hold our own and know what we truly love to do, we may be over the hill. Yet if that is what it takes, we must insist on following our heart still, so that our work will be our passion. Short of that, we will never be content and, with a "squatter" in it, the "room" of our work have no peace.

Our work is the soil that we till, plant in and harvest from, allowing us to go far in life. Plan well so that you have a fulfilling career and achieve the blissful balance of work and life, which is crucial to making this second little "room" of your soul elegant and stable.

The third "room" of your soul is that for your true self.

This may sound weird, for who else will it accommodate but yourself?

Yet it is a mistake that we often make: we put up with all we know but ourselves. We let the ideas of others crowd our mind, giving them a free rein — a wild ride on the highway of your mind; leaving little room for our own thinking. Our brain becomes a dumpster of the latest information and cyberspace clutter, with little room left for our own discovery. No matter how boisterously we talk, we are but regurgitating what has been said by others. Our opinions, however balanced they may sound, have all been voiced by others. We are keepers of nearly everything, but have lost the key to our own inner world, with no trace of us having ever truly lived in this last little "room" of our soul.

Such being the case, this little "room" can soundlessly collapse with the slightest blow, let alone any earthquake or crushing waves. Its paper-thin walls can be reduced to dying embers, snow on its roof a broth of slush, its floor swampy and its paper-lined windows shattered, revealing a true, sad inner space; a lonely soul quavering against the elements.

When sheltered perfectly in the three little "rooms," our soul is in its element. It is thus everyone's right and obligation, in such extraordinary times, to build a habitat for our soul. We may lack good looks, yet are bright and healthy. We may lack greatness, yet are no less noble. We may be imperfect, but will never cease our endeavor. We are mortal, yet artless and true.

Once solid, decent enough and well-stocked, such shelters for our soul can be expanded, with more "rooms" added in, until they become towering mansions. For the compass of our spirit can be as vast as the boundless universe.

紧张

　　一个有趣的游戏。两人一组，其中一人会拿到一些字条，上面写着字，表达的都是人们常有的一些情绪，比如高兴、漠不关心、嫉妒、疲倦已极……

　　拿到字条的人，要按照字条上的指示做出相应的表情和行动，让另外的那个人猜。

　　例如，甲看了看手中的字条上的字迹，沉思片刻后开始表演。先是豹眼圆睁，辅以一个箭步上前，右手揪住假想中的某人脖领儿，同时挥出弧度漂亮的左勾拳，击中那人腮帮……

乙在目睹了甲的表情和行动以后，也沉思片刻。然后大声说出他解读出的对方情绪——愤怒。

甲颔首道，基本正确。不过，我手中的字条上写的是"狂怒"。

乙说，嘿！如果是狂，你的这个表达等级味道尚欠浓烈。倘若换我，一般的愤怒就已达到这个档次。真到了狂怒阶段，还要加上怒发冲冠、拳打脚踢、暴跳如雷……

这个小游戏，说明人和人之间并不是很容易沟通的，人们通常按照自己表达情绪的方式来理解他人。

但人和人之间仍是可以沟通的，需要语言的帮助和长久的磨合。程度差异很大，可以一叶知秋，也可能盲人摸象。

我很喜欢玩这个游戏，可以更深刻地感知他人的内心，察觉人群的异同。正是这种无休止的差异，造成了人的丰富多彩和无数悲欢离合。

某次，我遇到了一位有趣的合作者，他是一位老板。

他拿了字条开始表演，目光炯炯，眉头紧皱，身板僵直，双手攥拳。

我绕着他走了三圈，思考不出他这番表演的内涵，求助道，你能不能示意得再明确些？

他是个好商量的人。思忖片刻后，加上了一个表情：嘴角紧抿……

我还是百思不得其解，只得求饶道，猜不出猜不出。我投降，快告诉我底牌吧。

他把字条递给我，上面写着"焦虑"。

想想也有道理，某些人焦虑的时候就是这副沉闷苦恼的模样。

第二轮测验开始。他看了一眼手中新的字条，开始表演：目光炯炯，眉头紧皱，身板僵直，双手攥拳。

我丧气地说，不行。再具体些。

他就又加了一个表情：嘴角紧抿……

天啊，我一筹莫展，甚至想：这一堆测验的字条里不会有两张"焦虑"吧？

我说，完了，我弱智了。请你告诉我吧。

他手心摊开，我看到了谜底"沮丧"。

沮丧是这个样子的吗？我不服气地说，你的表演有问题，沮丧的时候目光通常是低垂的。

但是，我沮丧的时候就是如此聚精会神的。他很诚恳地说。我只得服输。是啊，你不能否认有些人屡败屡战，永远目光炯炯。

再一次轮到他表演的时候，我格外当心。看到他拿了字条，踌躇了一下，然后胸有成竹地开始演示。

目光炯炯，眉头紧皱，身板僵直，双手攥拳。

看到我的茫然愁苦的模样，他善解人意地加上了一个补充动作：紧抿嘴角……

我极快地调侃道，干脆杀了我。我无法破译你的密码。

这次轮到他吃惊了，说，我有那么神秘吗？其实，这一次，我表达的是一种很平和的情绪——"安静"！

我几乎昏了过去，说，您的大驾尊容居然能称得上是安静？我想，当你自以为安静的时候，周边的人绝不敢打扰你。

说者无心，听者有意。他静默了片刻，一拍大腿说，哦，你这样一讲我就明白了，为什么我以为自己温和的时候，大家依然说我严厉。

那一次令人难忘的游戏结尾有些苦涩的味道。因为我的这位朋友，无论他拿到写着怎样字迹的字条，他的表情都像一个模子里刻出来的。目光炯炯……嘴角紧抿……甚至当"爱情"出现的时候，他也如此刻板和冷峻。

我问他，你成家了吗？

他说，成了。但是又散了。

我说，还打算成吗？

他说，暂时没有打算。

我说，没有了好。

他说，你为什么这样说？

我说，我的意思是，你若不把表情修改一下，即使有了女朋友，也会莫名其妙地走开。

我后来同这位老板详细地探讨了他的表情。他说，我一个当老板的，哪能事事都流露在脸上，让人看个透明？我这是深沉。

我说，表情的僵化和不动声色并不能画等号。对家人和对谈判对手，哪能一样？周恩来可算是大家，他的表情就丰富得很，并非整天板着阶级斗争的脸。咱们常常羡慕外国的老板当得潇洒，其中重要的一点就是他们真实，当怒则怒，当喜则喜。况且，老板也是人，也有七情六欲。事业做得好，人也要活得自然、自在。

后来，我和这位老板进行了比较深入的谈话，才明白在他那千篇一律的面具之后，准确地说，既不是焦虑，也不是沮丧，当然更不是安静，而是紧张。

紧张，是现代人逃脱不掉的伴侣。

紧张的时候，我们的心跳加快、瞳孔变大、呼吸急促、血流湍急……我们的思索急迫而锋利，我们的行动敏捷而有力。

"紧张"这个词，很多年以前被写进一所著名大学的校训。我想，那时它一定是有的放矢，有着历史的必然性和辉煌的功绩。

时代在发展，如今，当我们不再从战火和铁血的角度看待紧张，紧张就有了更多值得探讨的意义。

短时间的紧张很好，会使我们焕发出非凡的爆发力。不过，世界上的事情，一蹴而就的肯定有，但终是有限，大量的成功孕育在日积月累的跋涉。紧张是一百米短跑，成长则是马拉松比赛。长久的紧张如同长久的鞭策一样，是不能维持的，它会导致反应的迟钝。紧张可以应对一时，却无法永恒。

紧张是一种无休止的激动，是一种没有间歇的高亢，是一种针插不进水泼不进的致密，是一种应急和应激的全力以赴。

你见过没有起落的江河吗？你听过没有顿挫的乐曲吗？你爬过没有沟崖的山峦吗？你走过没有悲喜的人生吗？

紧张是面具。紧张的下面潜伏着怎样的暗流？换句话说，什么导致我们长久的紧张？

紧张的人，思维是直线而不是发散的，因为他的注意力太集中了，心无旁骛。当我们的视野中只有一个目标的时候，它是收束和狭窄的（不是指远大的唯一的目标，是指运筹帷幄的策略）。我们的显意识之下是深广的潜意识。当紧张的时候，理智和经验就占据了上风，而人类在长久的进化中所积累的本体感觉被抑制和忽略。所以，紧张的人很容易累。因为他是在用百分之五的能力负载着百分之百甚至更高的压力，怎么能不累呢？

紧张的人其实是不安全的。他处于风声鹤唳之中，对自己的位置和处境有深深的忧虑。他大张着自己所有的感官——眼睛瞪着，耳朵张着，手脚绷紧，呼吸也是浅而快的，他的全身就像一架打开的雷达，侦察着周围的一草一木。

他因袭着以往的重担，关注着周围的一举一动，无法平和地看待他人和看待自己。紧张的人睡眠通常不良，因为在睡梦中，他也不由自主地睁着半只眼睛。

打个比喻，什么动物最易于紧张呢？通常一下子就会想起老鼠、兔子、麻雀之类的，大都是弱小的、谨慎的、没有强大的防御能力的生灵。如果是老虎、狮子、大象，甚至蟒蛇，我们想起它们的时候，可以觉得它们懒洋洋或佯装安宁，但我们不会浮现出它们是紧张的这样一个印象。在突袭猎物的时候，它们快则快矣，狠则狠矣，你可以痛恨它，但它依然是从容的，它们不紧张。

再举南极洲的企鹅为例，这些穿西服的鸟似乎也没有伶牙俐齿可供攻伐猎物与保障自身，胖墩墩的战斗力不强，但是，它们毫无疑问不紧张。不是来自它们自身的强大，而是没有人类的迫害和袭扰，它们尚不知"紧张"为何物。

所以，紧张不是强大，只是懦弱的一件涂着迷彩的旧风衣。

紧张往往使我们看问题的角度趋向负面。因为不安全，所以防御感强，假如在判断不清的时候，首先断定对方是有敌意和杀伤力的，考虑自己怎样防卫、怎样规避、怎样逃脱……紧张会使我们误会了朋友的友谊，曲解了爱情的试探，加深了创伤的痛楚，减缓了复原的时间。在紧张的时刻，决定往往是短期和激烈的。

紧张的时候，我们无法清晰地聆听到真实的声音，我们自身澎湃的血液主导了我们的听觉。我们看到的可能并非真实的世界，因为自身的目光已经有了某种先入为主的景象。我们无法虚怀若谷地接纳他人的意见，因为自己的念头依然盘踞在心。我们难以深刻地反省局限，因为注意力全然集中对外，内心演出了一场"空城计"……紧张如同凹凸镜一般，真实的世界变形了，让我们进入高度的戒备状态。

紧张的人，是很难和别人和睦相处的。紧张的人，通常落落寡合慎言忧郁。紧张的人，孤独寂寞。他们可以置身于灯红酒绿、车水马龙当中，但他们的心多疑多虑，缩成一块石头。

人们很推崇一个词——大将风度，我以为其中极重要的组成部分就是不紧张。每一行真正的高手，几乎都是举重若轻、温柔淡定的。草船借箭诸葛空城，功夫在诗外，无论形势多么危急，他们都成竹在胸。无论己方多么孤立，他们胜券在握。哪怕局面间不容发，他们都眼观六路、耳听八方，大将不紧张。

On Tension

Word guessing is a fun game. It can be played in pairs. One person will be given some slips of paper, each with a word describing various human emotions, such as "happy," "indifferent," "jealous," "exhausted," etc., and act out a given emotion with gestures and facial expressions, while the other guesses.

It sometimes goes like this: Person A, after taking a look at the slip of paper in his hand and pondering for a moment, takes a step forward, and with rounded eyes, grabs the imaginary collars of an imaginary person with his right hand, while swinging his left fist at an imaginary jaw...

Person B, observing the dramatic representation, similarly ponders for a moment, before loudly declaring — Anger.

Person A may reply, "Pretty close. However, the word on the paper slip is 'Rage'."

Person B will snap, "Well, your acting wasn't intense enough for rage. That was how I will act when I am just plain angry. When I am enraged, I'd blow my top, punch and kick, be mad as hops and menacing..."

It goes to show that people tend to interpret others' feelings according to how they themselves usually react, and that effective communication can be difficult.

Yet real communication is possible, with proper use of language and continuous learning. There can be a world of difference between those who communicate effectively and those who do poorly. The former pick up the slightest hint, sensing the advent of autumn in a single fallen leaf, whereas the latter often grope in the dark.

I like this game which is rather telling as to the workings of the human mind and how differently people express themselves. It is the diverse manners of expression, while making human interactions dynamic and colourful, that are often at the root of either consummate or failing relationships.

Once, I played this game with a partner who was a business-owner. When he started to mime his hints, he struck a pose of standing upright with an intense, fixed stare, knitted brow and clenched fists.

After pacing and circling him three times without a clue as to what he meant, I prompted, "A bit more explicit, perhaps?"

Obliging, he pressed his lips together...

Still clueless, I threw up my hands, "I give up. Not a glimmer of an idea. Tell me what it is."

He handed me the slip of paper on which was written "Anxiety."

With hindsight, I can see that some people do carry such a

solemn and agonized look on their face when they are anxious.

Then we moved on to the second round. With a glance at the slip of paper, he started again: standing upright with a fixed stare, furrowed brow, and clenched fists.

"No. You've got to be more specific," said I, rather frustrated,

He then pressed his lips together... Alas, I still had no clue and thought for a moment that both slips of paper might have the same word. "Beats me," said I. "I have no idea. Just tell me what it is."

He opened his palm and I saw the answer: "Frustration."

"How could that be?" I protested. "Something wrong with your acting. When people are frustrated, their eyes are downcast."

"But I always felt more focused when I was frustrated," said he in earnest. I had to admit that there are those who remain bright-eyed despite repeated sctbacks.

Then again, it was his turn to perform. I watched more intently. He picked up the slip of paper and hesitated for a moment before proceeding with an obviously assured air: standing upright with a fixed stare, knitted brow and clenched fists.

Seeing the perplexed and agonized look on my face, he pressed his lips again, as a considerate afterthought...

"This is killing me," I protested. "There is no way I can decipher your hints."

Now it was his turn to be perplexed. "Was it that hard to tell?" he asked tentatively. "In fact, the emotion I wanted to convey was the very peaceful 'placidness'!"

I nearly fell off my chair. "You call that pose of yours 'peaceful'? I guess when you thought you were in your peaceful mode, nobody dared to wave a hello!"

My offhanded remark put him in a pensive mood. He fell quiet for a moment and then, with a slap on his knee, divined,

"Aha! That's why everyone said I was so stern when I thought I was being rather cordial."

The memorable end of our word-guessing game that day was tinged with poignancy. This partner of mine showed exactly the same expressions for all the different emotions. He would strike the same pose, with rounded eyes, tightly pressed lips... Even for the word "love," he acted aloof and stony-faced.

"Are you married?" I asked him later.

"I was, but we split."

"Ever thought of trying again?" asked I.

"Not for the time being."

"Good for you, then," said I.

"Why did you say so?"

"Well, if you can't change the way you express your emotions, your next partner would also leave you after being confused by you."

Later on, we had a thorough discussion about his body language. He explained, "Being the boss, I can't wear my heart on my sleeve. I have to be imperturbable; a man of substance."

"Self-possession doesn't mean you must be stony-faced all the time," I offered. "We simply can't treat our family the same as we do the person across the negotiation table. The late premier Zhou Enlai was a masterful communicator; eloquent, cordial ways, and never a person with a perpetual poker face. We admire business executives with a certain charm and disarming manners. An important factor that contributes to such an impression is their emotional truthfulness — not hiding or feigning any emotions. After all, as humans, we all have the usual spectrum of emotions. Endeavouring for business success doesn't go against being a genuine human being."

A further conversation with him revealed tension, rather than anxiety, frustration or serenity, being behind his fixed, imperturbable mask; tension that is an inescapable companion of contemporary humans.

Tension causes our heart to race, pupils to dilate,

breathing to quicken, and blood to surge... We think faster, our mind becomes razor-sharp, and our motion swifter and more powerful.

"Tension" was written into the motto of a well-known college in China decades ago. Such a notion (with a hint for "vigilance") stemmed from the historical context and mandate of the school and contributed to its remarkable wartime success.

Times have changed. Nowadays, we seldom think of tension in the sense of battle-ready vigilance in times of revolution and war, but rather the other facets of tension worthy of our consideration.

Tension, for short durations, can be a good thing. It brings out extraordinary bursts of energy. However, success in any significant endeavour, with a few exceptions, requires persistent, accumulative efforts. Tension is a requisite for the 100-meter sprint. Yet life's journeys are more often marathons, for which tension is unsustainable.

Chronic stress, like endless prodding, only dulls our response and spontaneity.

Tension is relentless agitation, exultation without repose; chokingly intense. It is our body's stress response — urgent and all-out.

Have you not seen rivers rise and subside? Have you not heard music soaring and swooping? Have you not crossed undulating hill country? Have you not had ups and downs in life?

Tension is a mask. Yet what torrents of emotions lie behind it? In other words, what makes us incurably tense?

When someone becomes tense, he is focused, oblivious to distraction, and his thinking linear, not lateral. In his narrowed and narrowing vision, he sees the single goal (tactical and no longer holistic or strategic). Lying beneath consciousness in his mind is the vast, powerful subconscious. However, when is tense, his rational faculty takes over, while his proprioception — the unconscious perception of movement and spatial orientation, a product of evolution — is suppressed and dormant. That's why we easily feel exhausted when tense. As we use only the conscious in coping with our enormous stress, leaving much of the powerful subconscious unused.

A tense person is seized with insecurity. He is paranoid, sensing danger lurking all around him. All his senses are on high alert — eyes peeled, ears pricking, fists clenched, and breathing shallow and fast. He feverishly sniffs round for any scent of trouble, like military radar scanning for impending assault.

He is burdened by his own past foibles, forever watchful, and never able to consider others and himself in a fair light. A tense man sleeps, proverbially, with one eye open, invariably suffering from sleep deprivation.

For comparison, what species in the animal kingdom are the most prone to tension? First come to mind are the feeble, skittish and vulnerable critters, such as mice, rabbits and sparrows. When tigers, lions, elephants, or pythons are mentioned, we are put in mind of their lazily lying about; being relaxed and disinterested, and anything but tense. Even when they are stalking prey, they have this eerie calm air about them, though nonetheless fast and fierce.

The penguins in the Antarctica, waddling about like little portly figures in tailcoat, do not have sharp beaks or claws to ward off predators. Yet they are without doubt not skittish, thanks not to their superior power, but to the fact they have so far been spared of human slaughter or harassment. They have yet to experience tension.

Therefore, tension is but a camouflage of feebleness. When we are tense, we tend to have a negative view of the world. Feeling insecure, we are wary and on guard. When in doubt, we err on the side of caution — assuming hostility and deadliness of our adversaries and plotting our defence; our fight or flight. We mistake friendly gestures, miss the cues that someone is taking a shine to us, and suffer intensified pain and slowed healing. When we are tense, we tend to make rash decisions on the spur of the moment.

When we are tense, we are less attuned to the voice of truth; deafened by the pounding of our own heart. Our perception may be far removed from the reality, coloured by our preconceived ideas. We fail to listen with humility and tolerance, because we are so full of ourselves. We fail to introspect, as our attention is all directed outward. We have a twisted view of the world, as that seen in distorting mirrors, and become alarmed.

A tense person finds it hard to get along with others. He cuts a solitary figure; glum and sparing of words. He is woefully lonesome, for even while sitting in the lap of luxury, or amidst the usual hustle and bustle, he is consumed with edgy suspiciousness and his heart as hard as stone.

"Being in full command" has become a much admired personal attribute. To me, its most important facet is calm and composure. Nearly all who excel in their own trade have an air of unruffled masterfulness about them, often with a countenance between gentle and calm in expression. The legendary strategist Zhuge Liang, of the ancient Three Kingdoms Era, for example, was able to pull off such feats as "capturing arrows by fooling enemies with boatloads of straw," or "dispelling an enemy attack by deceiving them into thinking the empty fort was full of ambushes," all by being supremely calm and self-assured, no matter how perilous the situation was. Assured of their inevitable success, they are superbly calm; nothing escapes their notice; they are in full command.

第二志愿

人们常常把所有的注意力都集中在第一志愿上。这些年，随着考试严酷性的不断升级，关于填报志愿的说法，也越来越霸道了——那就是全力以赴关注你的第一志愿。某些大学的录取人员公开宣布，我们是不会录取第二志愿的学生的，因为你的热爱不够专一，录来也学不好的。

高考形势特殊，僧多粥少，对于学校的取舍，旁人不好议论是非。但我以为，如果把高考报志愿的经验推而广之，把第一志愿至上，扩散成人生选择的一大信条，就有商榷的必要了。

人生的选择绝少是唯一的。

听一位美国心理学家讲座，谈到男女青年挑选恋爱对象时，他说，如果你在读大学的时候，一眼扫去，本班级上的异性，有三分之一以上可以成为你的配偶候选人，那么……

讲到这里，说是悬念也好，说是征询民意也好，他成心留出一个长长的停顿，用苍蓝的眼珠扫视全场。台下发出汹涌的低语声，均说，那他就是一个神经病！

异国的心理学家抖抖肩膀说，喏！那他或她，就是一个心理健康的人。这观点有点好玩，也有点耸人听闻，是不是？当然，他指的寻找伴侣，是在大学校园内，智商和背景有大的相仿，并不能波及整个社会，说某个男人觉得与世上三分之一的女人都可成眷属，才属正常。

但这一论点也可以说明，既然结为夫妻这样严肃的问题，都不妨有一手或是几手打算，那么，在其他场合的选择，当有更大的弹性。

当孤注一掷地把自己的命运押在某个"唯一"头上的时候，我们实际上处于自我封闭和焦灼无序的状态，内心流淌的是自卑和虚弱。以为只有这狭窄的途径，才是抵达目的地的独木桥，无法设想在另外的情形下，还有道路尚可通行。某些人的信念虽执着但脆弱，难以容忍自己的不成功。由于太惧怕失败的阴影了，拒绝想象除胜利以外，事态还同时存有一千种以上黯淡的可能。他们能够采取的自卫措施，就是放下眼帘。以为只要不去想，不良的结果就可能像鬼魅，只能在暗夜中游走，不会真的在太阳下现身。

于是每当选择的关头，我们可以看到那么多人鸵鸟似的奋不顾身，色厉内荏地跑跳着。到了没有退路的时候，就把小小的脑袋埋入沙堆。他们并不仅仅骗别人，首先的和更重要的，是用这种虚张的气势，为自己打气加力。他们拒不考虑第二志愿，觉着给自己留了退路，就是懦夫和逃兵。甚至以为那是一个不祥的兆头，好像夜啼的猫头鹰，早早赶走方平安。他们竭力不去前瞻那潜伏着的败笔和危险，好像不带粮草就杀入沙漠的孤军。即使为了应付局面多做准备，也是马马虎虎潦潦草草，虚与委蛇地写下第二、第三志愿……不走脑子，秋水无痕。不敢一针见血地问自己，假若第一志愿失守，能否依旧从容微笑？

可惜世上的事情，不如愿者十之八九。当冰冷的结局出现时，很多人就像遇到雪崩的攀缘者，一堕千丈。此刻，你以前不经意间随手填写的第二志愿，就像保险绳一样，在你下坠的过程中，有力地拽住了你，还你一方风景。

惊魂未定的你，此时心中百感交集。被第一志愿抛弃的巨大失落使百骸俱软，无暇顾及和珍视第二志愿的援手。你垂头丧气地望着崖下，第一志愿的游魂还在碎石中闪着虚光，有人恨不能纵身一跳，以七尺之躯殉了那未竟的理想。即便被亲人和世俗的利害，劝得暂且委曲求全，那心中的苦郁悲凉，也经久不散。

第二志愿如同灰姑娘，龟缩在角落里，打扫尘埃，收拾残局，等待那不知何日才能莅临的金马车。

其实人的才能是多方面的，守节般地效忠第一志愿，愚蠢不说，更是浪费。候鸟是在不断地迁徙当中，寻找自己的最佳栖息地，并在长途艰苦的跋涉中，锻炼了羽翼。在屋檐下盘旋的鸟，除了麻雀，还能想出谁？

寻找第二志愿的过程，实质上是对自己的一次再发现。除了那最突出、最显著的特点之外，我还有什么优长之处？第一志愿和第二志愿之间，可否像两位相得益彰的前锋交互支援？我还有哪些潜藏着的特质，有待发掘和培养？平日疏忽的爱好，也许可以在失落中渐渐显影？

第二志愿的考虑和填写，也许比第一志愿的取舍更艰难。惟妙惟肖地预想失败，直面败后的残局和补救的措施，绝非乐事，但却必要。尝试着在出征前就布置退却和迂回的路线，并在这种惨淡经营的设计当中，规划自己再一次崛起的蓝图，是一种经验，更是勇气。

也许是因为害怕面对这种挫折的演习，有人惊鸿一瞥般地拟下第二志愿，并不曾经历大脑深远的思考。他们以为这是勇往直前背水一战的魄力，殊不知暴露的只是自己乏于坚忍和气血两虚。

不可搪塞第二志愿，它依旧是人生重要的选择，是你面对逆境的备份文件。它是进可以攻退可以守的支撑点，它是无惧无悔的屏障，它是一个终结和起跑的双重底线。

或许有人以为，有了第二志愿第三志愿……人就易颓败，多疏忽。这是一个谬论。亡命之徒不可取，它使人铤而走险，一旦失利，便是绝望与死寂。不妨想想杂技演员，有了保险绳的时候，他们的表演会无后顾之忧，更精妙绝伦。

在填写第一志愿的时候，把其后的每一份志愿也都认真地考虑，这是人生不屈不挠的法门之一。

Second Choice

People often focus exclusively on their first choice. Students preparing for the National Higher Education Entrance Exam, for example, work all out to get the scores required by their first choice school or program. The fiercely competitive nature of the exam is such that some colleges openly declare they won't consider those selecting them as a second-choice. Their rationale: students who are just not in love with them won't do well if they are admitted.

Given the vast number of applicants competing for limited spots, focusing on your first choice may indisputably be the way to go. However, to apply this universally to all scenarios in life, putting such an emphasis on the first choice, is rather questionable, if not outright wrong.

In life, we are seldom stuck with having only one choice.

I once attended a talk by an American psychologist who, while commenting on dating choices, said if someone at college believes over a third of his or her classmates of the opposite sex can be their potential spousal choice, after a cursory look at them, then...

He paused for a deliberately long moment, either for suspense or to gauge reaction. As his grey eyes roved across the room, there was a wave of murmurs, "...He must be a psychopath!"

The psychologist shrugged, "No. He or she is perfectly normal and mentally balanced." This was rather intriguing, if not entirely shocking. Of course, the context was college students of comparable levels of IQ and background. It would indeed be odd if this sort of statement was made by a man about women in society at large.

It goes to show that if we are willing to contemplate more than one option even for such a serious matter as selecting a marriage partner, we can certainly be more flexible with our choices in various other scenarios.

When we throw our lot with a certain "only one," to the exclusion of all other options, we become introspective; growing ever more anxious and out of sorts. Consumed with self-loathing and feebleness, we make ourselves believe that we have made the right decision, oblivious to possible alternatives. We can be stubborn in our conviction, yet brittle, and cannot stomach any defeat. We refuse to imagine there can be a thousand other outcomes that are as respectable, though not as glamorous, as an absolute win. We look the other way, thinking that the less-desired outcome could be swept under the carpet, as long as they are shut out of our mind.

Thus, so many are given to running about madly like startled ostriches when asked to consider various options, and burying their heads in the sand when cornered. Such agitation reveals nothing but their lack of courage and confidence. They refuse to consider plan B, brushing it off as a sign of cowardice and surrender. They even regard having a backup choice as bad omen, like owls hooting in the still of night, to be shooed away so that all is quiet and well. They banish any signs of foreboding, like an army marching into the desert oblivious to impending perils and disaster. They may offhandedly throw in a second or third choice, merely for the sake of filling the blank spaces, without giving them any serious thought. They dare not ask themselves point-blank what if they fail to get into their first and only choice school. Would they smile or grimace?

Yet, your second choice, one that you might have left there casually, may actually save the day when you fail at your first. When life throws you a curveball, as it does nine times out of ten, your plan B will prop you up and open up new possibilities for you, like the life-saving rope to the climber when he is knocked off his feet in an avalanche.

Being rejected by your first choice school may cause a minor meltdown. You feel a tumult of emotions; powerless and even incapable of scrambling for your second choice. Your dream, as if something with a faint sparkle that has fallen off the precipice, flickers in the rubble. Crestfallen, you sense unrelenting pain and despair which could have easily made someone hurl themselves off the cliff to be reunited with the fallen dream, too, if not for the timely coaxing and advice from their loved ones. All the while, the second choice is there in limbo, to collect dust and wither; biding its time, like Cinderella for the uncertain prospect of riding the gold carriage.

In fact, our talents are multi-faceted. Focusing on our first choice, to the exclusion of all other options, is not only witless but also a sheer waste. We must dare to explore other options, like migratory birds that travel enormous distances for ideal breeding and wintering grounds, growing powerful wings in so doing; rather than sedentary sparrows, flitting here and there, never far away from the eaves under which they nest.

Finding the right second-choice schools is a process of self-discovery. What strengths do you have other than the most obvious? Can your efforts at getting into the first choice compliment those for your second? What are your hidden qualities that can be highlighted or further developed? What are your extracurricular pursuits that have been neglected, but may be appealing in light of your failure?

Thus, deciding on a proper second choice can perhaps be tougher than on the first, for you have to envision failure and plan for its aftermath. Yet, it is crucial, though by no means pleasant. It requires sophistication, and above all courage, to map out your retreat and turnaround in the event of failure, before you even start your journey.

Some are fearful of such a thorough exercise based on the assumption of failure. So, they put down their second choices in the blink of an eye, without so much as a thought. Such feigned resoluteness, like that in mounting a last-ditch attempt, only exposed their lack of genuine resolve, conviction and competency.

A second choice is nonetheless a critical choice, a plan B in the face of adversity; definitely not something to fiddle with. It offers at once a reprieve and a base to launch your comeback, eliminating the need for panic or regret. It marks the end of one endeavour and the start of another.

Some believe that with second or third choices to fall back on, one may become slack and lapse into mediocrity. This is a fallacy. In fact, when someone is cushioned with backup options, like an aerial acrobat with safety harness, they will more likely execute stunning and perfect performances, without worrying for fatal falls, whereas the reckless who are out on a limb can only despair.

So, when you have decided on you first choice, give serious thoughts to all other options, too. This is a sure-fire approach to strive and excel.

你不能要求没有风暴的海洋

痛苦和磨难，是人生不可分割的一部分。只有接受这一事实，我们才能超越它，更加看清生命的意义。

你说你不要这些苦难，那么生命也就失去了框架。很多自杀的人，就是因为没有理会这种意义，一厢情愿地认为生命是应该只有甘甜没有挫败的。然而生命的常态，其实就是平稳和深邃，还有暗流。在最深刻的层面，我们不单与别人是分离的，而且与世界也是分离的，兀自踽踽前行。

生命的每一步都带着人们向死亡之境跌落，不要存在幻想，这才让你比较持久稳定，安然地居住在孤独中，胸中如有千沟万壑、千军万马。只有接受这一事实，我们才能超越死亡，腾起在空中，看清生命的意义。

有一次，到沙漠中间的一个城中去，临行之前和当地的朋友联络。她不停地说，毕老师，你可要做好准备啊，我们这里经常是黄沙蔽日。不过，这几天天气很不错，只是不知道它能不能坚持到你到来的那一天。

我有点纳闷。虽然人们常常说，"您的到来带来了好天气"，或者说，"天气也在欢迎您呢"，谁都知道，这是典型的客套。个体的人是多么渺小啊，我们哪里能影响到天气!

不过这位朋友反复地提到天气，还是让我产生了好奇。我说，不管好天气还是坏天气，我们都不能挑选。天气是你们那里的一部分，就是黄沙蔽日，也是你们的特色啊。

说者无意，听者有心。后来，这位朋友对我说，她听了我的话，就放下心来。我很奇怪，因为自觉这番话里，并没有多少劝人安心的含义啊。她说，我们这里天气多变，经常有朋友一下飞机就抱怨，闹得主客都很尴尬。

我说，坏天气也是大自然的一部分，就像每个人的生命中都必定下雨，某些日子势必黑暗又荒凉。就像你不可能总是吃细粮，那样你就会得大肠癌。你一定要吃粗纤维。坏天气、悲剧、死亡、生病，都是生命中的粗纤维，我们只有安然接纳。

你不可能要求一个没有风暴的海洋。那不是海，是泥潭。

No Sea Without Squalls

Pain and suffering are integral to life, a fact we must reckon with before we can have a clear, transcendental understanding of the essence of living.

You want none of the pain and suffering in life, you say. Then it will be a life untethered to reality. Not knowing this, many who ended up killing themselves had wishfully thought that their life should have been a bed of roses without any setbacks. Life is both humdrum and profound, a placid river with dark undercurrents. In essence, we are all alone as we trudge our way through life; alienated from others and the world.

Each step along the way, life gets us closer to death. Discard any fancy notion purporting otherwise, and you will be better off, with lasting sereneness and content in the solitude of living. You will have inner strength and munificence in spades. Only when we come to terms with this basic fact can we rise above the scourge of death and have an elevated, clear view of life.

Once, I travelled to a town in the middle of a desert. When chatting with a friend there before the trip, I was warned: "Ms. Bi, you must be prepared for the desert dust that can hang in the air for days on end. We have been lucky to have had a spell of good, clear days. But no guarantee it won't change."

This baffled me. For people would customarily say, "You have brought good weather here." Or "We have good weather in waiting for you...," though everyone knew they were only well-meaning platitudes. An individual is too infinitesimal to have an impact on the weather.

However, after she mentioned this several times, I felt compelled to respond, "We can't be choosy about weather, good or bad. It is a natural feature of your area, even if the dust in the air can be thick enough to block out the sun."

My casual remark meant much to her. She later told me that she was relieved after I said that. I was surprised, for whatever I had said wasn't exactly meant to pacify. She went on to explain that since the local weather was so changeable, they often had visitors who were grumpy the moment they landed, which made everyone feel awkward.

I said that bad weather was part of nature, as suffering is part of living. Days of rain and woe are inevitable in everyone's life. As with our diet, we need plenty of fibre that comes from whole grains, not the usual refined grains, or else we risk getting colon tumour, among other things. Bad weather, illness, personal tragedy or near-death experiences in life are what high-fibre is to a healthy diet. We must accept them with aplomb.

You can't expect a sea voyage without squalls. If you do, you might as well go for a paddle on the pond.

生当做瀑布

世界上百分之八十的峡湾在欧洲，而欧洲的峡湾主要在北欧，北欧的峡湾则主要在挪威。峡湾的英文名是Fjord，有时特指的就是挪威的峡湾。

挪威南部的大西洋海岸线呈不寻常的曲折，多条宽阔的"海流"蜿蜒伸展到内陆达一百五十千米。峡湾的水非常深，一般都在几百米，最深达到一千二百米！两岸的山峰动辄也是千米高，万丈绝壁紧紧钳住一泓蓝水，这水还会随着潮汐一呼一吸，是不是有一种诡异的壮观？

峡湾里瀑布之多到了令人眼花缭乱的程度，可以说千米之内必有瀑布，常常是一眼望去，三四条瀑布同时跌落九天，细者如银丝，粗者如白绫。从北部的瓦伦格峡湾到南部的奥斯陆峡湾，车行之处，无数大小瀑布如万马奔腾。一条接一条，呼啸着喧哗着溅入峡湾，构成烟雨迷离彩虹飞架的仙境。

如果我是水，做哪里的一滴水呢？做藏北高原狮泉河的一滴水吗？那里太冷了。做大海中的一滴水吗？海啸壁起的时候，杀人夺命，造孽深重。做黄河中的一滴水吗？虽然历史久远，然携带泥沙太过劳累，不得休息。做南极的一滴水吗？虽然洁净，但万古不化的寂寞，也令人怅然。

思前想后，最后做了一个决定——生当做瀑布。瀑布的前身是小溪，无拘无束地跳跃和畅流。小溪们汇聚在一起，就长了能耐和勇气。人多力量大，水丰好办事。同心协力找到腾空而下的山岩，嘻嘻哈哈地纵身一跃，快乐地自高处跌下。水珠们拿着大顶叠着罗汉，倒栽葱地撞向深处，被风扯出透明的旗帜，在飞翔中快乐地撒欢儿。

瀑布没遮拦地降到了谷底，反倒安静了，变成了一汪小小的泉。如果有幸在挪威做了瀑布，通常不会旅行太远的行程，就被峡湾收编了去，成为海的一部分。

如果我是一滴水，纵是一滴普通的水，也希冀着跌宕起伏和波澜壮阔，也渴望游弋和携手，那就做一次瀑布吧。

Oh To Be a Waterfall

Eighty percent of the fjords in the world are located in Europe, while those in Europe are mostly in Northern Europe, and those of Northern Europe are mostly in Norway. The native term for narrow sea inlet — fjord — has been adopted by the English, either specifically referring to the Norwegian fjord, or sometimes referring to narrow inlets in general.

Part of the Atlantic beach of southern Norway is a series of unusual twists and turns, the manifold wide oceanic currents penetrating as far as one hundred and fifty kilometres inland.

Meanwhile, the cold water of the fjord strikes deep, usually reaching several hundred meters below sea level, the deeper fjords sometimes running up to one thousand and two hundred meters below sea level.

Likewise, the mountains on either side of the shoreline tend to run to a thousand meters — in height! What one would describe as a ten-thousand-feet high wall encircling a cup of blue water! Not any cup of blue water, mind you, but water that rise and fall with the tide!

Certainly a mysterious grandeur!

As to the number of waterfalls within a fjord, it is simply beyond count! One could safely say that you could run across a waterfall for every thousand-meter that you cover. You could raise your eyes and easily catch sight of three or four waterfalls tumbling helter-skelter down the sky, some slender like silvery skein, others an outpour like a splash of white silk.

All the way from the Varanger Fjord up north to the Oslo Fjord down south, our car went past countless waterfalls big and small that flashed by like teams of race horses, one following closely upon another, as in a fairy scene of a rainbow flashing by with a lot of stern and strum.

If I were a drop of water, where and what would I want to be?

A drop of water in the Lion Spring River in North Tibet? Too cold up there.

A drop of water in the boundless sea? In a sea storm, the swollen waters could kill, and killing is sinful.

A drop of water in the Yellow River? It has a long history, true. But having to carry sand is exhausting.

A drop of water in the Antarctic? Well, the hygiene is taken care of. But think of the everlasting solitude. Isn't that intimidating?

Looking at the problem from all sides, I finally came to a decision — living, I would like to be a waterfall.

The antecedent to the waterfall is the little stream, jumping up and down happily with its playmates.

The little streams join together and become more daring.

As the saying goes: More people — greater strength! So, more water — things get done!

The little streams get together and find a hanging cliff — up they jump and down they go, laughing all the way. Meanwhile drops of water, like rolling stones, tumble downwards, screaming wildly all the way.

Once down, the waterfall is silent, becoming a little stream. If it is lucky enough to have landed in Norway, then it does not need to go far to be absorbed into a fjord and become part of the sea.

If I were a drop of water — just ordinary water — I would still look to being part of a heaving wave, to be part of the action — in a word, to be a waterfall, even if only for once in a lifetime.